Meeting Louis
at the Fair

The Projects & Photographs of **Louis Clemens Spiering,** *World's Fair Architect*

Meeting Louis At The Fair

©2004 Carol S. Porter

All rights reserved

Virginia Publishing Co.

P.O. Box 4538,
St. Louis MO 63108

(314) 367-6612

www.stl-books.com

Book cover and interior design by Michael Kilfoy and
Bruce Burton of Studio X, St. Louis, Missouri
www.studiox.cx
Front cover photograph of Louis Clemens Spiering,
courtesy of The Sheldon Galleries.
Back cover photograph taken by Dan Dreyfus in Spiering's sunken
garden at Waterman Place and Union Boulevard, St. Louis.

ISBN: 1-891442-22-8

Library of Congress Control Number: Pending

Edited by Laura Fister and Julie Stevenson

Meeting Louis
at the Fair

The Projects & Photographs of **Louis Clemens Spiering,** *World's Fair Architect*

Carol S. Porter

Virginia Publishing   St. Louis, Missouri

For

Howard Porter

Louise and Wilbur Shankland,

my parents

and

Wilma Guyot,

my friend

Contents

Introduction

A few years before his death in 1912, Louis Clemens Spiering completed a monumental pencil and pastel panorama titled "The Architectural Apotheosis of St. Louis." This now-lost work depicted buildings "from Indian tents along a lonely river to the magnificent World's Fair Buildings and daringly predicted structures yet to come." It must have been stunning. Spiering's mastery of presentation drawings dated back to his prize-winning student days at the Ecole des Beaux-Arts in Paris. What buildings from the fair did he choose to illustrate in the "Apotheosis"? Would he have included his own work?

Unanswerable questions such as these plague every historian, especially one who apparently set off with a different goal only to become captivated by the subject matter. A short memo dated November 11, 1997 in the cluttered Spiering file at Landmarks Association's office stated that Carol Porter "is writing a musical about Louis Spiering and the Sheldon" for which we had provided background. The Sheldon presented a variation on that theme in October of 1999 with "Reclaiming a Lost St. Louis Treasure" consisting of lectures on Spiering by Carol Porter and Esley Hamilton interspersed with songs by Franz Schubert and Hugo Wolf. By now Carol was immersed in what would be four more years of research.

The result is singular. This is not just a book about the short life and career of a romantic subject and his ethereal contributions to the St. Louis World's Fair. It also provides valuable insights into the cultural life open to an exceptional German-American family, the rigors of the proper architectural training abroad and the competitiveness and jealousies apparently inherent in the profession. Spiering's story opens just as the long-awaited Eads Bridge is dedicated in a city still recovering from the divisiveness of the Civil War. By the time it ends, St. Louisans have come together to celebrate one of the only international expositions to achieve worldwide acclaim and financial success.

We probably will never be certain just what Spiering contributed to that fleeting world of magic, but we can indeed be better stewards of his surviving projects built outside the gates. Interest in returning the now-forlorn Carnegie Branch Library in Soulard to active use would be a perfect outcome of Carol Porter's comprehensive and persuasive publication.

Carolyn Hewes Toft

November 2003

Preface

Images of the St. Louis World's Fair of 1904 have been fixed upon my mental landscape longer than I can remember—but surely dating back as far as the fair's golden anniversary, celebrated the year I turned six.

Growing up here in the 1950s and '60s, I counted Forest Park as my recreational destination of choice. A trip to the Zoo or the Muny Opera was a big treat for a kid from the suburbs. My favorite, though, was the motorboats on the lake. What anticipation as we sputtered along that sunny, southward tack away from the boathouse, into the mysterious, cramped reaches of a cobwebby overpass, around a bend, into a canal, beneath a bridge…finally emerging on the glorious expanse of the Grand Basin.

There, even as a third-grader, I was awed by a sense of place. My historian father had made sure I knew that when I traveled on this body of water, I floated above the epicenter of that storybook land of long ago: the St. Louis World's Fair of 1904.

The fair entranced me. Proudly I learned its lore: the ice cream cone, the hot dog, the song. Our fair even had its own movie! I pored over black-and-white photographs of the huge white palaces that had risen over the Grand Basin, and learned that they were nothing but plaster, a substance called "staff." And that the majestic stone Art Museum, still standing sentinel over the water, was the only palace built to survive.

By whatever age I later happened into conversations about the fair with my young friends, I discovered that they, too, knew these facts. It was a kind of regionalized osmosis.

Since then, the St. Louis World's Fair of 1904 has only gained in fascination and sentimental appeal to those who live in its sponsoring city. Witness the shelves of books and monographs: World's Fair statistics and specifics have been chronicled, the exposition's political, sociological and cultural implications scrutinized. Lavish picture books have been published, fair trivia recorded, fair souvenirs catalogued.

This book is about none of these things. *Meeting Louis at the Fair* recreates the Louisiana Purchase Exposition through the eyes of one of its architects, examining the buildings he designed—most of them a departure from the rococo style of the better-known grand palaces—and the forces that brought them into being. It's a coming-of-age story as well, following the path of a young architect on his first professional assignment: to create an ethereal fantasy world, a sort of Edwardian Disneyland…in fact, a mammoth profit-making machine, animated by real-life, hard-nosed St. Louis mercantile aristocracy. Meeting Louis at the fair, we watch him meeting the realities of his notable, though brief, career.

I first came across Louis Spiering on an afternoon in 1997 while researching the history of the Sheldon Concert Hall in St. Louis, a 1912 structure that is a marvel of acoustical integrity. At the time, I was a member of a small a cappella choral group preparing a concert of early twentieth century popular music to be performed at the Sheldon, one of our favorite venues. Needing a script, we wondered if we might find inspiration in the history of the building, its stunning auditorium and its architect. Who was this Louis Spiering? Details were scarce, so I set off to the Missouri Historical Society library to investigate.

That's where I encountered Spiering—a World's Fair architect, as it turned out, who had helped design some of the very waterways I remembered from childhood. He was not the elderly personage I somehow had expected, but rather a handsome and impossibly young man of 37 when he died of cancer, seven months before the completion of his master work, the Sheldon.

Reading his obituary, I was struck by Spiering's impressive family connections (the extended Bernays clan, an intellectual German-American family, was prominent in St. Louis from 1855 to 1920 or so, influential in journalism, literary criticism, music and medicine); Spiering's impeccable education (Berlin and Paris, culminating in a diploma from the Ecole des Beaux-Arts); and his achievements during his final years in St. Louis (designs for the Soulard branch of the St. Louis Public Library, the original St. Louis Artists' Guild clubhouse, multiple residences in Compton Heights, the Central West End, University City and Webster Groves…and, of course, the Sheldon, designed as the first home of the Ethical Society of St. Louis).

I read on. The list of Spiering's honorary pallbearers was a who's who of St. Louis architects of the era: Klipstein, Eames, Mauran, Ittner, Link, Robinson, Brueggemann, LaBeaume. The funeral addresses bespoke a love and universal admiration for the young man that transcended clichéd funeral oratory.

By the time I left the library that afternoon, I was reeling. Here was a story that grabbed me on many levels. Beyond the obvious World's Fair connection, it combined my affection for music and music performance, involved my love of historical research, played on my long-standing appreciation of architecture and historic preservation and took place in one of my favorite eras, the early twentieth century. At the center of the drama was a sympathetic, tragic figure—bright, talented, doomed. Absolutely dedicated to his craft, Spiering lived out his final days directing the construction of the Sheldon from his deathbed. I felt a tug; I had to know more about this man.

As my research progressed, I realized that Spiering's brief St. Louis career, 1902–1910, was bracketed by monumental ephemera: staff and sound waves. The experience of purely transmitted sound is still enjoyed by audiences at the Sheldon. But the plaster magic of the World's Fair is accessible only via photograph. So when I eventually learned that Louis Spiering had taken photos at the fair, I recognized a defining moment: once again, he had circled me back to 1904. What would his photography reveal?

Spiering's photos, published here for the first time, are preserved in an album he titled, "A History of the Louisiana Purchase Exposition— St. Louis, Missouri, 1902–1904." The photographs are the chronicle of an artist intent on documenting his work. Many of the subjects we've seen before, but there's much that's new. Spiering's camera shows us close-ups that no other photographer had reason to record, small buildings long forgotten and vistas composed to offer pointed commentary.

Louis Spiering attached no text, no labels, no dates. The significance of his photos can be divined only by one who has dug into the particulars of his work at the World's Fair. Their artistry, however, finds a wider audience, and their overall imagery offers still broader appeal to everyone who has been enchanted by this mid-American Atlantis, the splendid lost city in Forest Park.

St. Louis County, Missouri
June 2003

Acknowledgments

Though my search for the elusive Louis Spiering began in a library in 1997, it blasted into orbit a little more than a year later when, acting on a hunch, I called a phone number in Burbank, California, and located Spiering's only remaining relative: his niece, Wilma Guyot. The daughter of Theodore Spiering, an internationally famous violinist and symphony conductor who was Louis Spiering's older brother, Wilma never knew her uncle—she was living in Berlin and not quite six when he died—but grew up steeped in the history of the illustrious Bernays and Spiering families. Responding to her gracious invitation, I, too, gained a sense of that history from the moment I entered her tidy gray California bungalow. As the last of both lines, Wilma, then a vigorous 92, lived amidst the keepsakes and furnishings that had always been part of her life, accompanying the family back and forth across the Atlantic for decades: Papa's music stand; Uncle Louis' breakfront, purchased at a Paris flea market during his student years; armchairs, beautifully preserved, originally the property of Charles Louis and Josephine Bernays.

Much, however, had already been given away by Wilma and her late sister, Lenore, after painstaking research to find exactly the right home for each artifact. The cultural institutions of St. Louis are the richer for these sisters' understanding of their families' place in our history and their careful stewardship of precious memorabilia: the Bernays china may be seen on display at the DeMenil House, while a treasure trove of manuscripts and archival materials—notably Louis Clemens Spiering's World's Fair photo album—is available to researchers at the Missouri Historical Society.

A singular treasure has been the keen memory of Wilma Guyot, connecting me to several generations of Bernayses and Spierings with reminiscences and anecdotes that have brought them vividly to life. I could not have written this book without Wilma's historical contributions—or, I suspect, her encouragement over five years of a richly rewarding friendship. She is an inspiration in her own right. She has my love, respect and deepest thanks.

The path to publication has been strewn with generosity.

A general-interest feature writer has much to learn when taking on a topic in architectural history. I am grateful to Osmund Overby, professor emeritus of art history and archaeology, University of Missouri, for his guidance, and the unfailingly generous, cheerful and kind manner in which it was offered. He has given more than his share of time to the overall project. Help with specific sections of the book has come from several quarters. Architectural historian Richard Chafee, known for his extensive research of the Ecole des Beaux-Arts and American students who studied there, provided priceless insights into Louis Spiering's Paris experience. Marie-Laure Crosnier Leconte of the Musee d'Orsay, an eleventh-hour referral, took time from her own book in progress on American and Canadian students of architecture at the Ecole to share her research and send valuable materials on the Paris Exposition of 1900. Her contributions advanced my understanding of French architects assigned to the St. Louis World's Fair, and Louis Spiering's relationship with them. Professor Helmut Hirsch of Dusseldorf, Germany, has studied the life of Charles Louis Bernays for at least six decades. He honored me with his observations and assistance; Marianne Hirsch, his wife, gave me the benefit of her considerable investigation of Bernays genealogy.

Where would we be without libraries and archives? Accolades to these outstanding local resources and the archivists within, who disappear into the shadows and emerge with treasure: Missouri Historical Society (Kristina Gray Perez and Duane Sneddeker, as well as Dennis Northcott, Dina Young, Randy Blomquist, John Goaring, Jason Stratman and Ellen Thomasson—indefatigable, every one); Saint Louis Art Museum (Norma Sindelar); Saint Louis Public Library (Barbara Knotts, Suzy Frechette, head of the Fine Arts Department, and in the Department of Rare Books and Special Collections, archivist Jean Meeh Gosebrink, and Tom Pearson); St. Louis Public Schools (Sharon Huffman); Washington University Special Collections (Carole Prietto); Stephens College Archives (Bobbie Burk); and the Western Historical Manuscript Collection (Ann Morris, former director).

I am grateful also to the St. Louis County Library Central Headquarters for its fine microfilm collection as well as a library loan system that I nearly wore out.

Elsewhere in the country: Linda M. Kennedy of Buffalo and Erie County Historical Society; Thomas Flynn of Cathedral of Saint Paul

Archives; Alan K. Lathrop; Leah Deem of Madison County (Ill.) Historical Society; Janet Olson of Northwestern University Archives; Sandra L. Tatman of Philadelphia Architects and Buildings Project; and Jim Stangel of Riverbank Acoustical Laboratories, Geneva, Ill., have been of great assistance.

An erudite and patient group of interviewees enhanced my research. Executive Director Carolyn Hewes Toft of Landmarks Association of St. Louis, whose grasp of the interplay of architecture and politics throughout our city's history is unrivaled, has been immeasurably helpful, as has Esley Hamilton, preservation historian for St. Louis County Parks and Recreation Department. Dean Cynthia Weese of the School of Architecture at Washington University deserves my deepest thanks, as do Nancy and the late Richard Bliss, Robert Duffy and the late George McCue. Still more assistance came from the enthusiastic participation of: Elliott Chubb, the late Lee Chubb, Dan Dreyfus, Walter Gunn, Margaret and the late Martin Hasse, Joy Katzen-Guthrie, Jean Ferriss Leich, Andrew Raimist, Bill Seibert and Emily Toth. I received a warm welcome and priceless information from present-day Spiering homeowners Edward Carlson, David McCollum, Chuck Niesen, Eileen and Tom Swoboda, and Barbara and David Ware.

Louis Spiering was a member of both the Ethical Society of St. Louis and the St. Louis Artists' Guild. I am happy to report these organizations are alive and well, exhibiting today the same spirited graciousness that characterized them a century ago. I am grateful for their patience during my extended prowls through their archives. The Sheldon Concert Hall, Spiering's great and final work, also thrives in the capable hands of executive director Paul Reuter, Dale Benz and many others, including former director of The Sheldon Art Galleries Suzanne Pace and her successor, Olivia Lahs-Gonzales. I owe them deepest thanks for their continuing interest and assistance.

Extensive translation of German texts was entertainingly accomplished by Steven Rowan, professor of history at University of Missouri, another Bernays-watcher; as well as Jason Baker, Clare MacKenzie and Mecky Myers. I benefited from excellent technical help from Meghan Anglim, Whitney Braun and Janna Burkhart Williamson. Additional support, much appreciated, came from my office neighbors at ComTrol.

When the manuscript was complete and cried out for the tough love of a discriminating reviewer, I could not have asked for better than my dear friend Bill Mayhan. From his hands the manuscript went to Studio X, where designers Michael Kilfoy and Bruce Burton transformed it into the intelligently beautiful book you see now. My patient publisher, Jeff Fister, along with Laura Fister, Julie Stevenson and Eric Winters, all of Virginia Publishing Company, brought the entire project handily and sensitively to fruition.

I am blessed with family and friends who unfailingly cheered me on through what seemed an interminable gestation. I am grateful to every one, and offer special thanks to those who helped specifically in an astonishing variety of ways: Louise Shankland, Nancy and Eric Seiler, June and Ben Hilliker, Claire Watkins, Colin Porter, Charlie Kennedy, Carolyn Braun, Pat Corrigan, Nancy Evans, Tim Gardner, Ann Kehler, Maxine Stone, Elizabeth Brandt and Blair Rieckmann.

Finally, I thank Howard Porter, who has been all things to me during the creation of this book. I will meet you at any fair, any time.

Part One

Beginnings

Prologue

A Blend of Fact and Imagination

May 1879

Louis Clemens Spiering, age 5, crept into the parlor and looked about. It was still in disarray, with tables and chairs pushed to the far reaches of the long, deep room—moved aside to make room for the box that had held Louis' grandfather. The box was gone now, and with it the masses of white flowers and the crowds of people who had been coming in and out for two days, and who had all gathered around the box this morning to hear some men talk about Grandpa.

The small, dark-eyed boy had been chucked under the chin by many of these people, whom he recognized as frequent past visitors to the house on Chambers Street. "Guten tag, Louis," they would greet him, pronouncing his name Lou-ee, as did everyone he knew. Louis was accustomed to hearing his grandpa engaged in endless boisterous conversation about something called politics, conversations that grew loud and insistent on all sides, though rarely angry. They were usually punctuated with laughter. Sometimes Grandpa would step to the piano bench and bring the debate to an end with a flourish of Beethoven.

Louis Spiering, undated, age 4.
Boehl & Koenig, St. Louis.
Private collection.

But today's gathering was hushed. Though his grandfather was the center of attention as always, he lay silent as speakers called him "Colonel Bernays" and "Doctor Bernays," talking one at a time, in quiet, sad voices. They called him a patriot, a preserver of the Union, a model American and a paragon of German virtue. They spoke admiringly of his courage in the long-ago journey across the ocean, settling in a new and unfamiliar land. From time to time, Louis and his seven-and-a-half-year-old brother, Theodore, saw their pretty mama, wearing a severe black dress, raise a handkerchief to her eyes or mouth. Their grandmother, however, stood with a stony face listening to the men talk about Grandpa. Louis looked over at her likeness hanging on the wall—a relief sculpture of Grandmother Pepi in profile, a lovely, pert young woman with curls clustered around her ears in the style of many years ago. Sometimes Papa held Louis to his shoulders so he could extend a tiny index finger and trace the wondrously lifelike ivory outline of the curls. The likeness of Grandmother Pepi, with its dimension and depth, fascinated the small boy who loved to study pictures.

Next to Mama and Grandma were Aunt Thekla and Uncle August. After this lively brother and sister returned from the university abroad, they became frequent visitors to the home Louis shared with his mama and papa, grandpa and grandma and Theodore—racing in from their own brick house next door, which looked just like his, adding their voices to the babel of jokes, debate and shaky arpeggios from the other end of the house, the product of Papa's young violin students.

But then Uncle August began to carry in his doctor's bag, and with only a grin and a quick joke for his little nephew, would hurry up the long, narrow stairs to the bedroom where Grandpa now stayed all of the time, sleeping, or, with an inkwell and sheaves of paper scattered about the bed covers, writing newspaper articles. He would smile at Louis, and wave him into the room. "Here, Louis," Grandpa had said one day not long ago. "Come and learn something about Spinoza." Eager for one of Grandpa's stories, which usually contained many funny long words unfathomable in either German or English, Louis approached the bed. But Grandpa coughed violently and fell back against the pillows. "Run along, now, Punktchen," said Uncle August, "and when I come out I'll tell you about the horse I bet on at the track yesterday." Louis heard his mother's bleat of disapproval, answered with uproarious laughter from August as the door closed behind him. He thought he heard Grandpa chuckling weakly, as well.

Now a man unfamiliar to Louis was saying words that sounded more solemn than any he had heard. Many of the visitors closed their eyes and lowered their heads. But Louis noticed that Uncle August was not among them, that in fact he seemed to be curling his lip. When the young doctor met his nephew's gaze, he made a funny face, bugging his eyes. Louis noticed a slight, sharp movement, and saw Aunt Thekla poke an elbow into Uncle August's arm.
Then came beautiful music, as Papa's string quartet brought the assembly to tears with a wordless tribute to Grandpa. "It's Mendelssohn," whispered Theodore, who had begun studying with Papa and made no secret of his desire to join the quartet, the sooner the better. An elderly uncle, whom Louis had never met before today, began to sob and was helped, wailing, to the door.

And then it was over. "You will stay here with Mrs. Harris, liebchen," whispered Mama. "We will come back soon, and then there will be some cake for you." So the little dark-eyed boy watched as the lid was lowered over his grandfather, and all the rest of the people he loved formed a line behind the box and walked slowly from the parlor.

Chapter One

Growing Up on Chambers Street

In photographs, Louis Spiering nearly always turned his left side to the camera. His large, wide-set dark eyes, the legacy of his grandmother Josephine Bernays, are fixed on some point in the distance.

If focused directly on the photographer, his gaze is intense. It is easy to read into the handsome young face a trace of sadness, a whiff of mortality, and imagine that he had predicted his own early demise.

FIG. 1.1 *Louis Clemens Spiering in the drafting room, Department of Works, Louisiana Purchase Exposition. Spiering Album. Missouri Historical Society, St. Louis (MHS).*

However, most studio portraiture of the era forces us to read overmuch into the faces it records, for neither the technology nor the conventions of the day encouraged informal, relaxed poses. Not until we examine Louis Spiering's own photo album of the St. Louis World's Fair of 1904 do we see him captured in a snapshot, in what today would be called a candid (FIG. 1.1). And here we meet an altogether different persona. Standing at his drafting table in the World's Fair design department, his slight frame enveloped in a smock, he looks up from his work to engage the photographer. He is clearly on the verge of a grin and—reading into the subject again—full of mischief. In no other image of Louis Clemens Spiering is he more obviously his grandfather's descendant.

"Bernays came bursting in..."

Charles Louis Bernays (1815–1879) made a profound impression on everyone who crossed his path—especially his youngest grandchild. Louis Spiering was a 3-year-old when they met, upon Bernays' return from an extended stay in Europe. The lively, bewhiskered old man reassumed his place at the head of their three-generation household, and for the next two years, before he died

FIG. 1.2 *Charles Louis Bernays, undated, about age 25. Private collection.*

FIG. 1.3 *Josephine "Pepi" Bernays, undated, about age 42. Private collection.*

of coronary disease, Bernays (FIG. 1.2) was probably the dominant figure in Louis Spiering's life.

Charles Louis Bernays easily dominated any setting. And there had been so many! Some of them involved tales that were suitable for the ears of young grandsons: Bernays' boyhood with seven siblings on an estate in Oggersheim, Germany; his free-thinking Jewish parents' engagement of a Jesuit tutor; his early years studying law at Heidelberg University. From there Bernays could jump to his 1848 emigration to the United States, telling of the long journey across the Atlantic on the *SS Sea-Lion*, and another journey up the Mississippi River. How he and Grandma Pepi (FIG. 1.3) expected to remain in St. Louis, but settled in Highland, Illinois, barely outrunning two great catastrophes that beset St. Louis in 1849: a cholera epidemic and the great fire that destroyed the wharf and adjacent city.

Bernays might have spoken colorfully to Louis of his new life in the tiny German-Swiss community: establishing a brewery and operating a general store, making dangerous horse-and-wagon trips, fording swollen creeks and crossing the Mississippi River by ferry as he bought goods in St. Louis, shuttling them back to Highland for resale at a profit. And the birth of Louis' mother, Theresa (FIG. 1.4), in 1850, would make this tale intriguingly personal to the little boy.

Louis Spiering may even have been treated to stories of Grandpa Bernays' later life: his return to St. Louis to assume the editorship of the German-language newspaper, *Anzeiger des Westens*, his vocal support of President Lincoln and the antislavery movement in Missouri, his influence on and energetic devotion to the nascent Republican party, his appointment as U.S. consul to Zurich and later Helsinki. Decades after Bernays' death, an ancient contemporary capsulized the effect of this dynamo on any sphere he entered: "Bernays came bursting in, and things began to bubble!"[1]

An Old-World Radical

But the psyche and intellect of a preschooler were ill-equipped to entertain the details of Bernays' activities between the time he obtained his law degree and his hasty emigration to the United States. By the 1840s, young Charles Bernays—already having lost an eye in a duel with a fellow student—had gravitated toward liberal journalism. His restless personality was suited to the profession, and so was his satirical writing style. "The truth is that he could tackle the driest subject matter and interlard it with brilliant apperceptions,"[2] recalled a fellow journalist. That colleague was Heinrich Boernstein, publisher of a radical Paris-based newspaper called *Vorwaerts! (Advance!)* It had begun innocuously enough as a multinational cultural journal, but by 1844 was absorbed by a publishing group supporting the ideals of Friedrich Engels and Karl Marx. Charles Bernays, a frequent contributor, was installed as editor. In the columns of this newspaper, historian Steven Rowan states, "the outlines of scientific socialism, which is the Marxist term for Marxism, were first laid down."[3] Bernays wrote fiery pieces propounding the cause of socialism, and advocating the overthrow of monarchy. Eventually *Vorwaerts!* was shut down by the French government, officially on a

FIG. 1.4 *Theresa Bernays Spiering, 1868, age 18. Hoelke & Benecke, St. Louis. Private collection.*

licensing technicality but in truth to placate Prussia after a Bernays article that seemed to support political assassination. Marx and Engels left Paris, Boernstein agreed to withdraw from publishing in France, and Bernays, according to Rowan, took the fall and was sent to prison for two months. In the aftermath of his release, Rowan has recorded: "He worked off his prison experience by writing a book on penology so savage and bitter that not even leftists would publish it."[4]

Thereafter, Bernays and Boernstein kept a low profile in their suburban Paris compound, supporting themselves as correspondents for German newspapers. They spoke often of emigrating to America, and did so with their wives, children and thousands of other German freethinkers who fled Europe after the failed revolutions of 1848. Late that fall, the Bernayses and the Boernsteins shipped out of Bremen with 46 trunks, their radical German worldview and a store of resilience and ingenuity, which they applied to their survival in

FIG. 1.5 *1102-1104 Chambers Street. Louis Spiering's childhood home. Private collection.*

the raw Mississippi River valley.

Louis Spiering, at 3 or 4, may have been too tender for the details of his grandfather's final pre-emigration years. But certainly intimations were abundant in that chaotic household on Chambers Street in Old North St. Louis (Fig. 1.5). The Bernays/Spiering parlor, a gathering place for a stream of visitors from across the U.S. and Europe, was the scene of passionate political debate. Some of it was surely fodder for the essays and articles Bernays continued to write for the *Anzeiger* and the English-language *Missouri Republican*. Bernays, a talented pianist, was sometimes called upon to accompany performers visiting St. Louis. Indeed there were several under his own roof. His wife, the former Josephine Wolf, had been a singer and dancer who entertained in the French court of Louis Philippe. Now Louis' father, Ernst Spiering, a violinist and leader of the Spiering Orchestra, taught music lessons from their home. And Louis' older brother, Theodore, had shown prodigious musical ability and, barely into grammar school, appeared bound for the concert stage.

The Compound on Chambers Street

When Louis Spiering was three, and already inured to cigar smoke, doors slamming, shouts and laughter, musical instruments played or assaulted, the volume on Chambers Street increased. Grandpa Bernays' closest brother, George, a retired physician, bought the house next door. With him came his five children, the youngest a boy, Walter, just Louis' age, and the oldest a brother and sister of 23 and 22, whom Louis came to know as Uncle August and Aunt Thekla (FIG. 1.6 and 1.7). This pair could have been taken for a mythical being—male and female versions of the same person, with their quick and imperious manner and snapping dark eyes. Thekla Bernays was a ferociously bright young woman, college-educated in Illinois as well as Germany, who would become an essayist, interpreter, translator and, as *St. Louis Globe-Democrat* contributor, a probable facilitator of Louis Spiering's architectural career. Her brother, August Charles Bernays, had just returned from graduate surgical training in Heidelberg. Although he hadn't yet become a household name in St. Louis by virtue of his sangfroid and almost miraculous surgical expertise ("eyes behind his eyes, ears behind his ears…and lamps at the ends of his fingers")[5], his fondness for racehorses and his aggressively agnostic views, the wunderkind A. C. Bernays had been a legend in his own family since he began to speak, they claimed, at the age of eight months.

In the extended Bernays clans, scholarly brilliance and mental agility had been noted for generations. Famous British chemist Albert Bernays was a distant cousin. So was Sigmund Freud, whose mother and wife were both Bernayses. Often found among the males was a pervasive nervous agitation, likely to erupt in volatile, eccentric or erratic behavior. Such was the case of Charles Louis Bernays, A. C. Bernays and, a generation later, Edward Bernays (1892–1995), nephew of Sigmund Freud but better known as the founder of modern public relations in America.[6]

The female members of the family, other than Thekla, are much harder to trace. It seems incomprehensible that Theresa Bernays Spiering, daughter of an intellectual powerhouse, would not have had the benefit of higher education. One reason may be found in Bernays' chronic financial troubles and frequent moves throughout Theresa's childhood and adolescence.[7] Generally, the Bernays/ Spiering women present themselves in family reminiscences and in correspondence—both in and between the lines—as intelligent, capable, resourceful and astonishingly tolerant of their restless spouses, whose households they were obliged to

FIG. 1.6 *August C. Bernays, M.D., undated. MHS.*

FIG. 1.7 *Thekla Bernays, undated. MHS.*

FIG. 1.8 *Theresa Bernays Spiering, 1879, age 29. G. Cramer, St. Louis. Private collection.*

continually uproot and reassemble.

The small Bernays compound was part of a busy neighborhood; their homes were actually one larger structure comprising two townhouses, typical of the area. Directly across the street, fronting on 11th Street, was the North Presbyterian Church (still in use today as SS. Cyril and Methodius Polish National Church), turning to young Louis Spiering its long profile, an implacable and unyielding expanse despite its bank of windows. Two short blocks to the north was Webster School, a public grammar school.

As the 1880s began, Louis continued to grow in a typically German, family-centered household. He attended Webster School, and his education was supplemented at home—again, the German tradition. He studied the piano, and according to family members, played extremely well. Uncle August continued as a source of diversion and entertainment, eventually filling the void left by the death of Grandpa Bernays, whom he so resembled.

August Charles Bernays would gain fame as a pioneer in asepsis, and a celebrity in surgery. To his credit was a series of firsts: first successful surgery on an abdominal gunshot wound west of the Mississippi[8], first U.S. cesarean section for placenta previa, first U.S. total removal of the stomach.[9] The newspapers loved Dr. Bernays. Whether he was removing a knife from the throat of an amateur sword-swallower, or a bullet from the stomach of one of St. Louis' finest, his daring and resourcefulness made great copy. Reporters also flocked to quote his prognoses of high-profile medical catastrophes, such as his prediction of the ultimate fatality of the assassination attempt on President McKinley in 1901. Earlier that summer, his opinion on another subject made front-page news.

"WARNING TO OLD MEN," read the headline, "Dr. Bernays Thinks There Is Danger in Golf."[10]

The degree to which young Louis Spiering understood or appreciated the headlines is not recorded. He is more likely to have appreciated the attentions of a charismatic uncle who, having benefited from art lessons, could keep a lecture hall (or a small boy) spellbound as he illustrated anatomy, drawing simultaneously with both hands, each gripping a piece of contrastingly colored chalk.

Prelude to Berlin

The other dominant adult male figure in Louis' world on Chambers Street was, of course, his father, Ernst Spiering. Among the dark, animated Bernayses, Ernst stood out. Blond, blue-eyed and comparatively quiet, Ernst was born in Luebeck, Germany in 1845. As a boy, he had emigrated to the United States with his parents, but lost them both to yellow fever not long after the family disembarked in New Orleans. Left to his own devices at the age of 11, Ernst Spiering decided to support himself as a violinist. He was befriended by Robert Meyer, a New Orleans music director, and by the age of 17 was traveling to Cuba on concert tour. The following year he went to St. Louis, eventually meeting Theresa Bernays (FIG. 1.8). The couple married in 1869, and had three sons: Theodore, in 1871; Louis in 1874; and Ernst Paul, born in 1876, who died in infancy.

Ernst Spiering (FIG. 1.9) probably had very little time with his sons. He maintained the typically frenetic schedule of a musician, teaching and performing in several venues. He gave lessons in the family home, played in the St. Louis Philharmonic Quintette Club and led his own group, the Spiering Orchestra. The latter was quite popular, and enjoyed a tony social and civic following. "Of late years, no festive gathering in fashionable society was considered complete without the assistance of [Spiering's] orchestra," noted the *Missouri Republican*.[11] An 1875 newspaper account summarized by the journalist William Kelsoe

FIG. 1.9 *Ernst Spiering, undated. Boehl & Koenig, St. Louis. Private collection.*

FIG. 1.10 *Theodore Spiering, 1878, age 7. St. Louis. Private collection.*

reported a banquet honoring James B. Eads at the Southern Hotel, attended by St. Louis Mayor Joseph Brown, Illinois Governor John L. Beveridge, General William T. Sherman and D. P. Rowland, president of the Merchants' Exchange. "The music on this occasion was furnished by the Spiering orchestra, conducted by Prof. Ernest [sic] Spiering."[12]

Louis (left) and Theodore Spiering. Undated photograph by West End Gallery, St. Louis. Private Collection.

As a teacher, Spiering must have been gratified to discover that his outstanding student was his own son Theodore (Fig. 1.10). By the age of 8, Theodore was playing publicly in solo recitals, collecting press clips and showing every indication of an unusually promising career. Theodore's parents plotted a course for the young prodigy: if he lived up to expectation, he would go to Germany to study with one of the world's greatest violin teachers, Joseph Joachim. In the meantime, in 1886, he traveled to Ohio and boarded there while attending the Cincinnati College of Music and preparing with the renowned Henry Schradieck, former concertmaster of the Leipzig Gewandhaus.

It is likely that Theodore, when departing for Cincinnati, saw his father for the last time. The senior Spiering died on August 15, 1887, of cancer. Theodore was not quite 16. Louis was 13.

Theodore returned home, briefly taking on his father's violin students. But Ernst had left a sizeable estate[13], and the family elected to carry out the original plan for Theodore's education and training. On July 10, 1888, they boarded the steamer *Weser* in Baltimore, bound for Bremen, Germany. A passenger list names Theresa, Theodore, Louis and their grandmother Josephine Bernays.

There is only the sketchiest surviving account of Louis Spiering's adolescent years in Germany. In Berlin he completed classic German preparatory education by attending the Real Gymnasium. Then, in 1891 he matriculated as a student of architecture at the Imperial Institute of Technology, Berlin. In 1892, having completed his technical training in architecture, he was ready to gain practical experience. Theodore was already back in their homeland, so again following his older brother, Louis returned to the United States.

The Chicago Years

In 1892, Louis Spiering found himself employed in the Chicago office of architect William A. Otis. Spiering almost certainly had not evolved a master plan of making his career debut as a St. Louis World's Fair architect ten years down the road in 1902. But if he had, he couldn't have chosen a better year, city or employment with which to lay the groundwork.

Otis (1855–1929) put Spiering immediately in touch with the tradition and educational philosophy of the Ecole des Beaux-Arts in Paris, the world's premier educator of architects. Otis had studied there in the 1880s. And living in Chicago gave junior draftsman Spiering (FIG. 2.1) a front-row seat for the World's Columbian Exposition of 1893, a Beaux-Arts inspired extravaganza that became the model for at least a half-dozen subsequent American fairs, including the one in St. Louis.

Reminiscing about the Chicago fair in 1895, William A. Otis called it "so wonderful as to be simply overwhelming."[1] Why? "Because it was beautiful. Architecture, landscape gardening, painting, sculpture, all the arts represented—were in accord and each one dependent upon and helping the other."[2] The Chicago fair, crowning Jackson Park on the shore of Lake Michigan, was a buttercream fantasia of palaces, fountains and waterways (FIG. 2.2). Most significant, it presented itself as a civic entity—that is, an instant city, a City Beautiful, testimony to a growing belief among architects such as Otis that an urban environment could be designed and constructed all of a piece, with every element contributing to an aesthetically harmonious whole.

America was ready to embrace such a notion. Having grown in population, industry, wealth and culture in its

FIG. 2.1 *Louis Spiering, 1893, age 24. W. J. Root, Chicago. MHS.*

first 125 years, the country wanted civic spaces and structures that reflected its status and power. Pierre L'Enfant's layout of Washington, D.C., with its axial boulevards and plazas, had provided an early example of urban planning. Now this Paris-inspired vision was popping up again in the imaginations of young American architects who, in growing numbers, had traveled abroad to obtain their education and training at the storied Ecole des Beaux-Arts. Returning as "Beaux-Arts men," they put their stamp on late nineteenth-century American cityscapes with ordered, balanced classical public buildings and residences. By the time Louis Spiering sailed back to the country of his birth, examples of the grand new order were rising, such as the Boston Public Library (McKim, Mead and White, 1888–1895, FIG 2.3) and the Art Institute of Chicago (Shepley, Rutan and Coolidge, 1892).

Architectural historian Richard Guy Wilson has said that the City Beautiful movement crystallized with the World's Columbian Exposition of 1893.[3] Most of its principal architects were *anciens eleves*, or alumni, of the Ecole des Beaux-Arts. Louis Spiering happened to arrive in Chicago in time to assume a place in the line of succession to the architectural aristocracy that was focused, for the moment, on the "Great White City," the exposition. It is remotely possible that through Otis, Spiering became linked to the "dean of American architects," Richard Morris Hunt. If a direct link cannot be proved, the succession still suggests the workings of the Ecole-driven architectural old-boy network, and its influence on the way young architects may have obtained sought-after world's fair work.

The Ecole Lineage

Richard Morris Hunt (1827–1895) was the first U.S. citizen to study at the Ecole des Beaux-Arts. In 1857, he

opened the first American *atelier* (design studio),
based on the teaching model of the Ecole.
During the next four decades, he rose to national
prominence as he designed a number of American
landmarks, including Lenox Library and the
Tribune Building, both in New York City. Hunt
became the darling of Gilded Age industrialists,
and was responsible for several of their lavish
estates, such as the Vanderbilts' Biltmore in
Asheville, N.C.; and their seaside "cottage," the
Breakers, in Newport, R.I. One of Hunt's final
commissions was the gleaming domed Palace of
Administration at the Chicago World's Fair.

FIG. 2.4 *William A. Otis, architect, ca. 1878 . Otis was Louis Spiering's first employer, 1892–1895. Winnetka Historical Society.*

Another American to enroll in the Ecole, a
generation later, was William Otis (FIG. 2.4). His
years of study coincided with those of a talented
young French designer, Emmanuel Masqueray.
After returning to the U.S., Otis joined the
Chicago office of William LeBaron Jenney,
one of the architects responsible for the new structures then
rehabilitating the city after the great fire of 1871. By 1886,
Otis was made a partner, and the firm was rechristened Jenney
and Otis. In 1889, Otis opened his own office.

Meanwhile, Masqueray, winner of two coveted prizes at
the Ecole, embarked on further architectural study in Italy. He
eventually moved to New York City to join the firm of Carrere
and Hastings, a powerhouse in the making. (Architects John
Carrere and Thomas Hastings, too, had studied at the Ecole
contemporaneously with Masqueray and Otis. Their firm is
responsible for the monumental New York Public Library,
completed in 1911.) After about five years with his fellow
anciens, Masqueray moved to the firm of Richard Morris
Hunt, where he produced several designs for the Breakers.
After a year with Hunt, Masqueray, in 1893, established his
own office and *atelier* in New York City. In 1901, Masqueray
would be named chief of design for the St. Louis World's Fair.

How does Louis Spiering figure into this litany of begats?
We can guess that Otis was acquainted with his fellow *ancien*
Masqueray, whom he may have introduced to Spiering. We do
know that Spiering and Masqueray were already acquainted
when the chief of design offered Spiering a job in 1902, for

FIG. 2.5 *Orrington Lunt Library. William A. Otis, architect. Campus of Northwestern University, Evanston, Ill. Northwestern University Library.*

Spiering wrote his mother: "Last Saturday Masqueray wrote me a very nice letter from St. Louis in which he offered me a good, even an excellent position."[4] This is clearly an update to a possibility already under discussion; Spiering's semi-informal referral to Masqueray by the surname indicates an existing familiarity (on the part of his mother, as well). In addition, Spiering alludes to "a position" in "St. Louis," with no need to specify the fair.

This existing link between Masqueray and Spiering is important. A world's fair design post was a plum for young architects, inspiring some would-be candidates to creative acts of self-promotion, as we shall see. It is significant that Spiering, in contrast, was recruited by Masqueray. It is almost as if the talisman were placed in Spiering's waiting hand.

William Otis, in addition to making a possible Masqueray-Spiering introduction, may have provided the inspiration for Spiering to attend the Ecole des Beaux-Arts. On the other hand, raised in the Bernays-Spiering tradition of only-the-best-education-and-that-means-European, Louis Spiering may have held the Ecole as his long-term ambition. In the meantime, he demonstrated his commitment to education by studying painting and watercolor in the evening school of the Art Institute of Chicago.

On the Job

Meanwhile, Spiering's professional development was nurtured in his years with William Otis. Entering the firm as a draftsman, he was later made superintendent. As Spiering came on staff, Otis was plunging into the design of the Orrington Lunt Library on the campus of Northwestern University in Evanston, Illinois (FIG. 2.5). Otis designed it to serve several functions: those traditional to a library (reference, periodical and reading rooms), plus an assembly hall and an arts room/ meeting place for the University Guild, which populated it with marble busts and full-figure classical statuary. Lunt Library was the first of several "multiplexes" that Spiering would professionally encounter or create. Most notable was his Gauntlett Hall (1907), the music conservatory at Stephens College in Columbia, Missouri, into which he incorporated practice rooms, performance space and administrative offices, all crowned by a third-floor gymnasium. Gauntlett Hall was demolished in 1995.

Spiering's involvement with the Lunt Library is evident. A copy of the general specifications, housed in the Northwestern archives, bears penciled notations for changes and additions, unsigned but obviously written in Spiering's hand. He must have had difficulty keeping track of the specs, because a warning appears on the cover, in the same handwriting: PROPERTY OF ARCHITECT!!! NOT TO BE TAKEN AWAY FROM THIS PLACE!!![5]

Orrington Lunt Library was dedicated on September 26, 1894. It was designed, William Otis said, "with the possibility of small and repeated additions."[6] Otis created a center pavilion with two wings, of adapted Italian Renaissance design: "extremely satisfactory in its application to the practical points of construction, while its classic details seem most in harmony with the refinements of literature and art."[7] He declared the principal artistic feature to be "the large semicircular porch with its delicate Ionic columns of very beautiful proportion."[8] By 1926, Northwestern University had outgrown Orrington Lunt Library, despite the careful planning of its architect, and a replacement was proposed. The old library building was recycled through succeeding decades to accommodate evolving university needs. As of the year 2002, Lunt Hall, meticulously restored, was the home of the university's mathematics department.

FIG. 2.6 *Auditorium Building (right) and Congress Hotel and Annex, Chicago, Ill. Louis Sullivan, architect. Library of Congress, Prints and Photographs Division, Detroit Publishing Company Collection.*

As the library was going under roof, William Otis wrote his client at Northwestern to assure him of the firm's vigilance: "My own architects' superintendence is <u>much</u> more thorough and strict than usual since either myself or my men are at this building <u>every day</u> from one to four hours."⁹ Spiering probably made the trek from the office at Monroe and Dearborn in Chicago to Evanston several times a week.

Living in and traveling about Chicago gave Louis Spiering daily updates on stimulating new developments in both architectural style and substance. The drawing boards of designers such as William Le Baron Jenney, Daniel Burnham and William Holabird were producing phenomena that Spiering had not observed in Europe: skyscrapers. The development of structural steel had given American architects the ability to create high-rise buildings with multiple windows, and the inspiration to ornament the exteriors with broad lines that suggested the internal structure. Jenney, in 1884, was the earliest to do so, with his ten-story Home Insurance Building, commonly designated the first skyscraper. During Spiering's years in Chicago, he was eyewitness to the construction of successor landmarks such as the Monadnock Building of Burnham and Root/Holabird and Roche, and the Reliance Building by D.H. Burnham and Co.

And then there were the creations of Dankmar Adler and Louis Sullivan (1856–1924). Sullivan, like Burnham, Holabird, Roche and William Otis, was a Jenney alumnus, an Ecole des Beaux-Arts dropout who had begun designing starkly simple residences and commercial buildings that he decorated with intricate organic-inspired ornamentation—blossoms and sinuous interwoven vines. Adler and Sullivan's Auditorium Building (1886–1890, FIG. 2.6) on South Michigan Avenue had just been completed, as had a residence on North Astor Street, the Charnley House (1891), by the young Frank Lloyd Wright (1869–1959). The simplicity of the latter and the lush decoration of the former startled Chicago architecture watchers, but to Louis Spiering's eye this fresh and exciting

work was surely recognizable as
cousin to the art nouveau and allied
Secessionist movements he had seen
gaining momentum in Europe.

The Home Front

While in Chicago, Louis Spiering
again lived with his mother and
brother, Theodore, at 3539 Michigan
Avenue. If he had any time for
diversion, he probably found his
family life nearly as invigorating as his
working world. Theodore had finished
his studies with the renowned Joseph
Joachim in Berlin, who helped him
acquire a rare circa 1729 Guarnerius
violin with which to begin life as a
musician in the United States. This he
did as a member and frequent soloist
with the Chicago Symphony Orchestra
under Theodore Thomas, giving his
family many opportunities to hear
him play in the opulent Auditorium

FIG. 2.7 *Theodore,
Frida and Lenore
Spiering, 1896. W. J.
Root, Chicago. Private
collection.*

Building that the orchestra called home. Theodore Spiering
remained in Chicago until 1905, shaping an ambitious
professional persona. He founded and directed the Spiering
Violin School from 1899–1902; and was a director of
the Chicago Musical College from 1902–1905. He also
established the Spiering Quartet, a stellar group of musicians
that traveled to major halls and tiny auditoriums throughout
the United States, playing more than four hundred concerts
during twelve years of existence.[10]

In October 1895, Theodore married his longtime
sweetheart, Frida Mueller of Cincinnati, also a descendant
of intellectual German Forty-Eighters. But Louis Spiering
was not present to celebrate their wedding, or the birth of
their older daughter, Lenore, the following year (FIG. 2.7).
Early that spring, Louis Spiering had concluded his work in
Chicago and crossed the Atlantic once again. His destination:
Paris and the Ecole des Beaux-Arts.

Seven Years in Paris

"Mr. Spiering, so far as known, is the only St. Louis architect holding a diploma from the Beaux Artes. [sic] There are twenty such in America."

— St. Louis Republic, **August 1, 1902**

Imagine a school so prestigious that any American student who simply passed its entrance examinations and attended a semester or so of lectures and corresponding lab work would later find his professional world parting before him like the Red Sea. Such was the luster of the Ecole des Beaux-Arts in the latter half of the nineteenth century. If a young man—the first young woman was not admitted until 1898—were to persevere through the four, eight, even ten years usually required to earn a diploma, he was nearly Pantheon material.

Imagine, too, arriving in Paris to storm this fortress equipped, perhaps, with preliminary instruction in architecture and a facility in French (if one were wise), but with little more beyond uncertainty. Such was the case with Louis Spiering, who presented himself to the Ecole on May 21, 1895, via a letter from the American Ambassador to France. Like any candidate—or *aspirant*, as they quickly learned to call themselves—Spiering had no guarantee of admission, or, if he succeeded, any assurance of earning a diploma at the Ecole. All he could count on was years of intense work in largely abysmal conditions. He was walking into an intellectual boot camp, architectural frat house, finishing school, Grand Tour and slum (Fig. 3.1).

Fig. 3.1 *Louis Spiering, 1897, age 23, as an Ecole des Beaux-Arts aspirant. Eug. Pirou, Paris. MHS.*

Affectionately
Louis
Paris. Dec. 1895,

FIG. 3.2 *Louis Spiering,*
1895, age 21. Private
collection.

Spiering's first item of business was the matter of those horrific entrance examinations: written and oral marathons testing, *en francais*, facility in mathematics, descriptive geometry, history, drawing and architectural design. Most *aspirants* took up to a year or so in Paris to prepare, and even then were likely to fail on the first try. Spiering, however, must have been supremely confident, for he elected to take the June 1895 exams (FIG. 3.2). Considering the intelligent grace with which he later earned commissions and accolades, carried out his design work and entered into the cultural life of St. Louis, one would expect to learn that Spiering breezed right through. He did not. Moreover, Louis Spiering failed the entrance examinations six times between 1895 and 1898, before passing on his seventh attempt in April 1898.*

The Ecole

Until 1865 and the establishment of the architecture program at Massachusetts Institute of Technology, American students who wanted formal education in architecture were forced to go abroad. Richard Morris Hunt was the first American to attend the Ecole des Beaux-Arts. His subsequent professional success and his Ecole-style design studio in New York City attracted attention and won followers. The numbers of American Ecole graduates grew, until by 1918, there would be approximately four hundred Americans who could say they had passed the Ecole entrance examinations.[1] Little in the American educational system prepared them for the experience.

The Ecole des Beaux-Arts was the French government-sponsored school of fine arts, situated on rue Bonaparte on the Left Bank of Paris. A venerable institution, dating to the seventeenth century, it offered programs in art, architecture

The author is indebted to architectural historian Richard Chafee, for his generously proffered analysis of Louis Spiering's student dossier. It is one of five hundred that Chafee, conducting doctoral research in the 1970s, studied in the records of the Ecole des Beaux-Arts, now housed in the Archives Nationales, Paris. Additional information about the Ecole cited in this chapter, except as noted, is attributable to Chafee's essay, "The Teaching of Architecture at the Ecole des Beaux-Arts." See The Architecture of the Ecole des Beaux-Arts, *edited by Arthur Drexler. 1977. The Museum of Modern Art, New York. Distributed by The MIT Press, Cambridge, Mass.*

and sculpture. Although a traditional school, in that it comprised a small campus, a faculty who taught a curriculum and held examinations, issued grades and eventually a diploma, the Ecole was nontraditional in the way it allowed students to advance through the school. The Ecole taught architecture on a point system. Students accumulated points with each passing grade in the curriculum, which included: theory of architecture, history of architecture, construction, perspective, mathematics, physics and chemistry, descriptive geometry, building law, general history and French architecture.[2]

Students also won points with each successfully completed *concours*, or architectural design competition. There was an order of progression: a *nouveau* (new student) entered the *deuxieme classe*, and after accumulating the prescribed number of points, was promoted to the *premiere classe*, where the cycle repeated. A student might go on to obtain a diploma, though not many did. Students could remain at the Ecole as long as they wished, advancing or not, until they reached the age of 30 and/or decided they had learned all that they could.

Projets and "Pigsties"

Much of the learning took place in the *atelier*, or design studio, and it was this institution that was most jarring, in fact and in theory, to incoming American students. The mostly off-campus *ateliers* were like architectural labs, where students completed all their projects and competitions. Each was headed by a *patron*, or master, an established architect who visited the *atelier* one or more times weekly to critique students' work. (The *patron* conducted his own practice elsewhere.) Many of these masters were themselves *anciens eleves* (former students) of the Ecole; a few were winners of the Prix de Rome, the Beaux-Arts' most prestigious honor. A genial competition flourished among the *ateliers*, and fierce loyalties pervaded each one.

Other elements pervaded the *ateliers*. Louis Sullivan, for six months an Ecole *eleve*, called his *atelier* "the damnedest pigstie [sic.] I have ever seen."[3] The typical *atelier* was a fourth- or fifth-floor walk-up in one of the Left Bank's seedier neighborhoods. (Think *La Boheme*.) Students worked in large, fetid rooms heated only by a sputtering coal stove, each drawing board lighted by candles stuck to its surface. Louis

Spiering, working in the *atelier* of Noel-Marcel Lambert, might have routinely dodged wet sponges hurtling through the air, traded *bons mots* or joined in whistled renditions of operas. As a *nouveau*, he may well have been subjected to a typical hazing, ordered to fight a duel, naked, with paintbrushes. He would have been called on to assist the senior *eleves* as their competition deadlines drew near, bringing reinforcements of cakes and pen nibs, stretching linen drawings over frames and delivering the precious *projets* minutes before the fatal hour.

Working cooperatively in this way was a novelty to many Americans. It provided all Ecole students with an understanding of good architectural design, as they scrutinized and debated any number of *projets* within the *atelier*. The occasional visits of the *patrons* were instructive, as well, though when they appeared, the *atelier* atmosphere was transformed into one of quiet respect.

Learning Architecture According to Plan

The Ecole philosophy regarded architectural design as a distinct, rational process. At its core was the plan—or perhaps "The Plan." *Eleves* learned that good design developed from the inside out, that above all a building must serve the purpose for which it was created. It is important to note that while the Ecole taught a process rather than a style, eventually the term "Beaux-Arts" came to suggest formal, balanced design owing much to classical examples from ancient Greece and Rome down through the Renaissance. Louis Spiering, while on faculty at Washington University, explained the reason for an emphasis on the classical: "We believe it to be…essential for the student in design to be taught an architectural alphabet, grammar and vocabulary as it is for the poet or writer of prose to become familiar with the elements of language. The beginner is taught the classic orders, not alone so that he may familiarize himself with the elements of Greek and Roman architecture, and in order to learn the names of the moldings so that he can speak intelligently of them, but also to train his eye to proportion."[4] Spiering himself rarely designed in the "Beaux-Arts style." Architectural historian Esley Hamilton has observed: "What Spiering got from the Ecole…seems to have been the freedom to design in whatever format he thought appropriate to the circumstance."[5]

An Opposing View

Certainly the Ecole des Beaux-Arts had its detractors. An
early one was Louis Sullivan, the iconoclastic architect whose
designs were just beginning to gain attention in Chicago
during Louis Spiering's years there. Sullivan spent about six
months as an Ecole *eleve* in the 1870s. His *Autobiography
of an Idea* paints an entertaining picture of his passionate
espousal of French educational philosophy and culture, and
an amusing account of his own transformation, by horrified
French classmates, from rough-hewn specimen into Parisian
dandy. Though enamored of Paris, Sullivan tells us, in the
end he had to listen to the voice within: "And there came
the hovering conviction that this Great School, in its perfect
flower of technique, lacked the profound animus of a primal
inspiration."[6]

Later critics of the Ecole would expand on Sullivan's
objections. Hugh Ferriss (1889–1962) became Louis Spiering's
most famous student from Washington University, known
internationally for his arresting drawings of 1920s and '30s
skyscrapers and his moody evocations of futuristic cityscapes.
(Ferriss graduated from Washington University in 1911 with
a B.S. in architecture. His father, Circuit Court Judge Franklin
Ferriss, resigning his place on the bench, had served as general
counsel to the Louisiana Purchase Exposition Company.)
Ferriss recalled his misgivings about the Beaux-Arts method of
instruction from his earliest days in the architecture program,
when students were directed to the library to find artistic
inspiration in the "masterpieces of the ages." There, studying
historic styles, he was distracted by an airplane passing
overhead. It triggered a nagging doubt: "Would the energy
expended in appreciation of architecture's yesterdays prove a
fatal subtraction from the energy needed to design for today?
How many admired archaeologists are influential designers?"
Shortly thereafter, he recalls, he wrote a "Student Manifesto":
"If we had been born beside the Aegean in the best century of
Greece maybe we, too, could have designed a Parthenon. But
yonder water is the Mississippi; no one frequents temples here
and now; if Ictinus were alive today, his buildings would not
be Parthenons."[7]

However, these radical opinions were in the minority, at least during the first decades of the twentieth century.[8] As more American universities established architectural departments through the latter nineteenth century and into the early twentieth, the trend prevailed: import a French *ancien eleve* to head or at least teach in the program. Thus grew the Ecole influence in the United States, and the inspiration for American diplomes such as Richard Morris Hunt and eventually Louis Spiering to establish *ateliers* in their home cities. Having grown accustomed to the intellectual ferment and creative stimulation of the *atelier*, as Richard Chafee has suggested, they felt deprived without it.

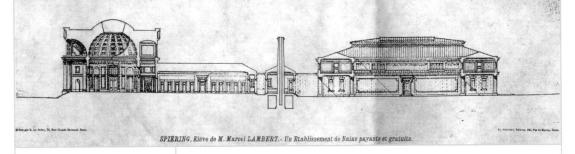

SPIERING, Elève de M. Marcel LAMBERT.- Un Etablissement de Bains payants et gratuits.

The Method

FIG. 3.3 *"Etablissement de bains payants et gratuits." Architectural drawing by Louis Spiering, ca. 1901. Spiering received a medal for this project. From* Les Medailles des Concours d'Architecture a l'Ecole Nationale des Beaux-Arts a Paris, Vol. III (1900–1901). *Private collection.*

The Ecole method of design began with simple exercises, such as planning and drawing a small portion of a building—an entry, perhaps. Students gradually acquired a kind of design vocabulary and the ability to pull quickly from this memorized catalog. As students progressed, the storehouse grew to encompass ever more complex design solutions. Their grasp of this process was tested over and over again in a series of *concours*, or competitions, held at regularly scheduled intervals.

To enroll in a *concours*, an *eleve* such as Louis Spiering would report to the Ecole and receive the program. It might be titled "Etablissement de bains payants et gratuits" ("A Bathhouse for Paying and Nonpaying Clientele," FIG. 3.3) or "un embarcadere sur un lac" ("A Landing-stage on a Lake")—though probably not, as later parodied by an architecture student of Spiering: "Bungalow for a Byzantine Bachelor with a Greek Soul, Mediaeval Morals, and an Ultra-Modern Income."[9]

The program set forth conditions: use, dimensions, site limitations, number of people expected to use the structure, by what means they might arrive (carriage, gondola, etc.). The *eleve* then entered an alcove for up to twelve hours, where he was said to be *en loge*, preparing a *parti* (preliminary solution), which he demonstrated in an *esquisse* (sketch).

While *en loge*, the *eleves* were allowed to confer with one another. However, they could see no one from outside the building, and as they left they registered their *esquisses*, and were not allowed to return. Thus committed to an original concept, the *eleve* carried a tracing back to his *atelier*, where he had a set length of time—from a week to three months, depending on the *concours*—to develop his kernel of an idea into a detailed presentation of plans and sections. After the deadline, a jury compared each entry with its original *esquisse*. Any variation and the student was disqualified as *hors de concours* (out of competition).

In the *concours*, Louis Spiering learned to work under pressure with speed and ingenuity...helpful to any professional, and especially to a future member of a world's fair design staff.

The Student

But Spiering was a long way from a *concours* as he struggled to pass his entrance examinations. What might account for his difficulty? His preparatory education, completed in German schools, may not have adequately prepared him for the differing French approach. Still, he was fresh from three years in the Chicago office of a Beaux-Arts *ancien*. Whatever the impediment, it was significant.

We know that Spiering was subject to migraines when under stress of prolonged study. He wrote his mother in 1899, the day after a mathematics exam: "I had one of my headaches....When I came home I laid me down on my ear to sleep" it away.[10] He was not one, however, to be sidelined by *la migraine*. In the same letter, he reported that despite the headache, he left the lecture hall after completing his exam for a chatty visit with his instructor in sculpture, not returning home until about 9 p.m.

Although he stood up to the headaches, Spiering was apparently no match for Cupid's arrow, and that may have affected his early performance at the Ecole. According to Louis

Spiering's niece, Wilma Guyot, the young man was smitten by
a Finnish student remembered only as "Sigrid." They became
engaged, and Spiering traveled from Paris to Finland to meet
her parents. But Sigrid eloped with her cousin, leaving behind
a filigreed gold bracelet, the gift of her devastated erstwhile
fiance. He never loved again, according to Mrs. Guyot,
although he was an object of interest not only to Washington
University female students but also to a devoted friend, Alice
Muench, who ministered to him during his final illness.[11] We
see Spiering in a studio portrait dated 5 September 1897,
transformed into a proper French gentleman *aspirant* with
an aggressively waxed moustache, looking stiff and tense in
his white tie and tails. In his right hand is a pair of white
kid gloves.

His Performance

Spiering wrote entertaining letters from the Ecole, but
only four of these survive, and none from the painful cycles of
disappointment and rededication that marked his first two and
a half years in Paris. On May 21, 1898, his perseverance was
rewarded at last, and he was admitted to the *deuxieme classe*.
Once an *eleve*, he outshone many of his American counterparts,
earning his diploma in about four years. At that time many
people never got a diploma, according to Chafee, and those
who did took longer than four years to go through the Ecole.

A letter dated October 1899 shows him unfazed and good-
humored after a grilling by his mathematics professor:

"In the oral examination he at first gave me a task in
analytical geometry with the resolution of integral equations,
etc. That went very easily. Then he asked one of those blasted
discussion questions....'Why does a pair of vectors not have
a resultant?'[12] I gave him the same demonstration I gave him
seven months ago, in response to which he interrupted me and
said, 'Sir, you told me the same thing seven months ago;
I know that there are those who do it that way, but I find it to
be absurd. I believe, sir, that we cannot see eye to eye.'
The entire hall laughed, since my colleagues were expecting
this show.

"At the end he gave me an assignment from mechanics
that I also did without hesitation. I was exactly 25 minutes
at the board, and when I left to get some fresh air, Dodge,

Parsons and other colleagues besides followed me out to congratulate me."[13]

Spiering's grades were good, and during his studies, he won four medals—top honors in the grading system. Two were for *modelage*, shaping clay into sculpture. Apparently a greater honor nearly came his way toward the end: "According to Lambert," he wrote, "I almost got a medal [perhaps for his diploma project], but that does not matter, since my friends Levi and Bans have one, which made me happy since they had a lot of trouble here."[14]

Diversions

Eleves did enjoy goodly chunks of time off between examinations and *concours*—allowing opportunity to explore European cities and countryside. Louis Spiering described the itinerary of one such trip through Italy and promised his mother to send his impressions. A natural outcome of these student trips, travel sketches were a means of sharpening the eye and recording the sights, which would be incorporated into the young Americans' future work when they returned home.

FIG. 3.4 *Arch of a typical entrance to the Paris Metro, ca. 1900 by Hector Guimard. Photograph by Kyle Griffith © 2000. University of Washington Libraries Digital Collections. Also see Fig. 6.6.*

Another popular distraction during Spiering's time in Paris was the great Exposition Universelle of 1900. Once again, Spiering got to watch the planning and development of a major world's fair; this one practically in the Ecole's back yard. He saw Paris torn up to accommodate the Metro system being readied for the fair, and the appearance of Hector Guimard's startling Metro entrances (FIG. 3.4) in the oddly playful/sinister art nouveau style that intrigued many Europeans and enraged still more. Spiering does not comment on the Metro installations, but other new structures caught his eye. "The new bridge, Alexander III bridge, and the two Beaux-Arts palaces are wonderful," he wrote. "Otherwise I have seen nothing noteworthy."[15] Indeed the spirit of the Pont Alexandre III with its elegant lampadaires would be evoked in the 1904 World's Fair, in Spiering's designs of bridges crossing the lagoons.

Paris is already like a street fair, he cautioned in this letter. Apparently he was besieged with guests that year, for he wrote that he had drawn up a mock business card (FIG. 3.5) in case wealthy acquaintances asked for him ("a steal, isn't it?" he commented wryly):

Louis C. Spiering
Interpreter
English, German, French
Terms whole day $10
half $5
and all expenses paid.

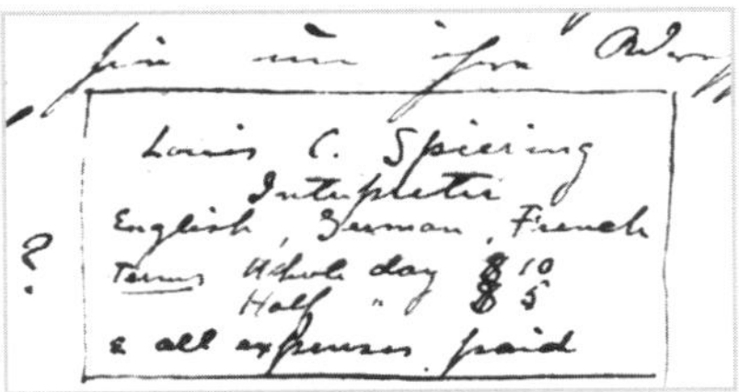

FIG. 3.5 *Letter from Louis Spiering to his mother, with "business card." Private collection.*

The Thesis

Students registering for the graduating thesis project were permitted to choose their subjects. In 1902, Spiering chose "A Mansion for a Rich Amateur of Music." Noel-Marcel Lambert, his patron, was reportedly so pleased with the project that he planned to exhibit it the following year in the Paris salon. It is unlikely that any drawings from the project survive, although a reproduction of the side elevation may be seen in a catalog published in 1905 (FIG. 3.6). According to the accompanying copy, written by George Julian Zolnay, a well-known sculptor of the day: "The liberal interpretation of Tuscan style in this design denotes not only the scholarly architect, but also the highly trained artist. This mansion, intended for a music lover, provides, in addition to the usual appointments of a fine residence, a large music room, a monumental hall for busts of famous composers and a library-museum for collections of old instruments and rare manuscripts."[16]

It is tempting to wonder if Spiering hoped that he—or perhaps his brother, Theodore, still a Chicago violin soloist in 1902—would someday be the wealthy music-lover occupying this house.

Adieu to Paris

Richard Chafee speculates that Spiering was being observed by "an important person" during his years at the Ecole. According to Chafee, Spiering's dossier contains "a letter from the Directeur des Beaux-Arts (i.e. the head of a government ministry, or perhaps number two in the ministry) to the head of the Ecole, who was a person lower in rank. The letter discreetly lets the Ecole know that Spiering has friends in high places." The letter, written in 1897, asks to be kept informed of Spiering's grades on entrance exams.[17]

FIG. 3.6 *"A Mansion for a Rich Amateur of Music,"* side view. *Diploma project of Louis Spiering. From* **Illustrated Handbook of the Missouri Art Exhibit.** *Courtesy of Special Collections, Olin Library, Washington University.*

We don't know who showed such interest at this point. But we can infer that Emmanuel Masqueray, his future *patron* at the St. Louis World's Fair, was keeping close tabs on Spiering's final performance in the *premiere classe*. Spiering wrote his mother on April 4, 1902: "Hopefully you have received my telegram of 1 April and know...I am at long last due for a diploma. Last Saturday Masqueray wrote me a very nice letter from St. Louis in which he offered me a good...position." The timing of these communications suggests that Masqueray had been waiting for confirmation of Spiering's diploma, and immediately wrote with a job offer.

Spiering took a four-week trip through Italy, and returned to Paris in May to receive his diploma. A final, almost giddy letter, dated July 8, 1902, mentions some of the highlights: "I have been continuously invited out. Today, for example, Fleury is giving me a grand dinner in Versailles, and before that I am bidding farewell to Lambert. Recently I was received into the Society of Architects Certified by the Government. It was the most lovely festival of my life: banquet at Ledoyen's, all the top architects were there, perhaps 80 to 100 of them, with champagne."

Then Louis Spiering traveled to Boulogne, where he boarded the *SS Blucher*, bound for the United States. He was about to take on his first professional appointment as a world's fair architect. He was pleased with the salary—about $48 per week—and no doubt with the honor. "It will only be hard," he commented, "to work eight hours and more a day in the dreadful heat of St. Louis."

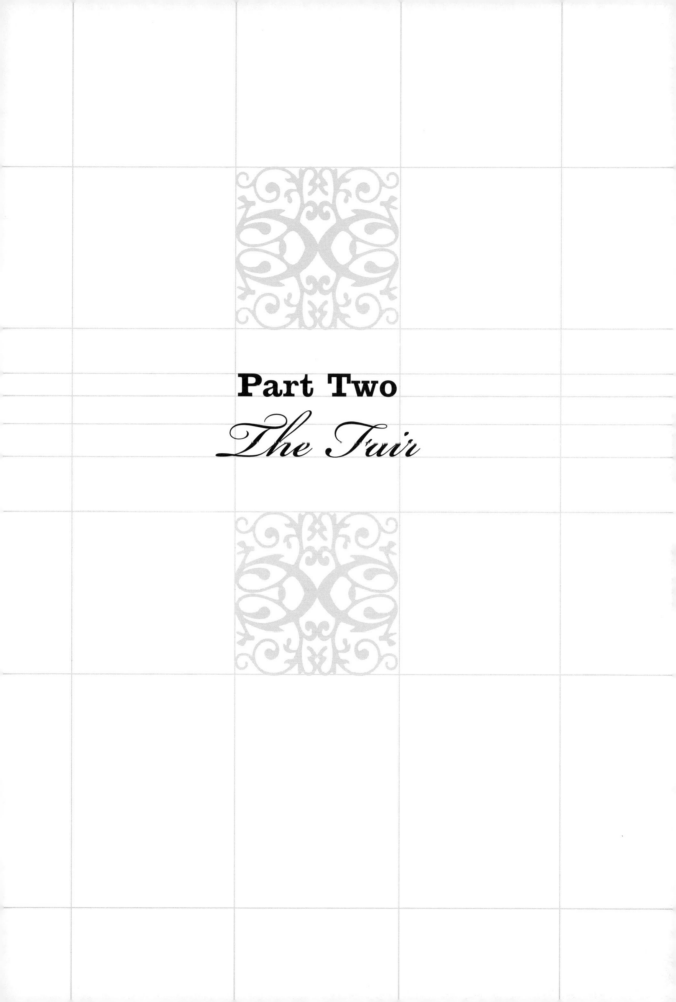

Part Two
The Fair

Interlude

Continuing in the Realm of Imagination

Mid-November 1902

Louis Spiering stood at a second-story window of the Administration Building of the Louisiana Purchase Exposition. Here, he was close to the far western boundary of the fairgrounds—all 1,200 or so acres of it. The Bureau of Exploitation had been booming the fact that the St. Louis fair would be larger than the Chicago and Philadelphia fairs combined. They hoped this impressive news would compensate for the delay of opening day. Now it was to be April 30, 1904—fully a year after the original date! Ah, well. The Chicago fair of 1893 had been delayed for a year, too, and still shone in the memories of millions.

Now, looking across the wasteland stretching to the east, Louis thought again that the august LPE Executive Committee had been rash to promise an earlier opening date. For nearly a year now, the fair's Division of Works had dispatched men, mules and machinery to tame this wilderness that was Forest Park. Hundreds of ancient trees had been felled, each yielding with a horrific crack, and then a thunderclap as trunk and crown smashed to the forest floor. They were dragged away, and their stumps blasted from the earth. Meanwhile, the River

*Emmanuel Masqueray,
Chief of Design,
Louisiana Purchase
Exposition. J. C. Strauss,
St. Louis. Cathedral of
St. Paul Archives.*

des Peres, a flooding nuisance, had been subdued and driven beneath the fairground through an ingeniously constructed wooden channel, a kind of river coffin.

Today the wonderland-to-be languished, ready to dissolve into an ocean of mud after the next hard rain. Louis sometimes felt as if the fairmakers had rewritten the creation story in reverse. Only the sight of enormous rising structures, swathed in scaffolding, far on the eastern horizon bore testimony to the potential of this busy, barren place. But Louis saw the promise; he understood and shared the vision of the two men most responsible for a transformation: Isaac Taylor, the St. Louis architect who headed the entire Division of Works, and Emmanuel Masqueray, Taylor's chief of design and Louis' immediate superior.

What an amusing and unlikely pair they made, Louis had thought, as he watched them studying Cass Gilbert's latest plan for Festival Hall earlier that morning. Grandpa Bernays would have written a satirical description of the two, describing first the fastidious Masqueray, no taller than five feet five, and then the burly, dynamic and perpetually rumpled Isaac Taylor, who towered over Masqueray by at least half a head.

Taylor had apparently been the uncontested choice for director of works, a position that placed him at the head of architects, engineers and laborers. In his early fifties, he had built a successful architectural practice since graduating from St. Louis University. Though his degree was in classics, he had entered the architectural office of George Barnett, where he learned his craft. Seven years later, he struck out on his own. Taylor's commissions ran more toward the commercial; his firm had designed the Planters Hotel, the Rialto Building, and the newly completed Bank of Commerce. He was a favored architect of the elite group of St. Louis businessmen who ran the city, and a friend of former Missouri governor David Rowland Francis, the equally dynamic organizer of the fair and president of the Louisiana Purchase Exposition Company.

Isaac Taylor also headed the Architectural Commission of the fair. These dignitaries represented the eight firms appointed to design the principal exhibition palaces that made up what Taylor dubbed the "Main Picture" of the fairgrounds. In their hands were the new century's temples—some of them acres in square footage— to Fine Art, Machinery, Transportation, Varied Industries, Electricity and Machinery, Education and Social Economy, Manufactures, Mines and Metallurgy, and Liberal Arts. Four of the firms, all with prior exposition experience, had been brought in from other cities: Carrere and Hastings, of New York; Cass Gilbert, St. Paul and New York; Van Brunt and Howe, Kansas City; Walker and Kimball, Boston and Omaha.

Then there were the local firms: Barnett, Haynes and Barnett; Eames and Young; Theodore Link; and Widmann, Walsh and Boisselier. Each firm would receive compensation of $10,000 plus a generous reimbursement of expenses. Taylor would coordinate the work of all and design a building of his own.

Louis had observed that the St. Louis fair planners seemed almost obsessed with comparisons of their fair with that of Chicago. Certainly the palace designs he had seen proved that the architecture, as well, would rival that of the competitor to the north. Louis laughed, remembering the disgust with which Louis Sullivan had cast aside the Chicago spectacle. What had he called it? A contagion? A virus that would set American architecture back fifty years? Sullivan had hoped that Chicago would spawn a new, uniquely American spirit and style of architecture, with his Transportation Building for the World's Columbian Exposition setting the standard. Instead, the designers had cleaved to Beaux-Arts classicism, mixing the architecture of eras and nations in a chaotic, rococo pastiche.

(Top) **Isaac S. Taylor, Director of Works, Louisiana Purchase Exposition.** *J. C. Strauss, St. Louis. From* Missouri's Contribution to American Architecture. *Private collection. (Above)* **David R. Francis, President, Louisiana Purchase Exposition Company.** *From* The World's Work—the St. Louis Exposition. *Private collection.*

The temporary material known as staff, a lightweight modeling medium of hemp fibers soaked in thin plaster of Paris, made it possible to construct baroque embellishments at relatively low cost. Thus the St. Louis fair designs—already sprouting domes, towers, turrets, minarets and porticoes beyond the wildest interpreting of Taylor's style criterion of "modified Italian Renaissance"—were to be fairly encrusted as well with sculptural ornamentation. Even now, pomegranates and cartouches had been ordered in by the carload from the fair's sculpture enlarging shop in Weehawken, New Jersey.

No, thought Louis. Sullivan would not regard the St. Louis fair kindly.

Though poor Masqueray had had nearly a year to regain his composure after walking into this horreur, his artistic soul suffered. He found it richly ironic that Isaac Taylor, his chief, had aroused the ire of some principal architects because he had curtailed the excesses of their designs. "The essence of good design is that a building reflect the purpose for which it was intended!" Masqueray recited, rhythmically snapping his yellow leather gloves against the palm of his left hand for emphasis. As the designers labored over linen drawings that stretched four, five, even six feet along their drafting tables, Masqueray paced among them. "Make it simple…always make it simple!" he implored.

Masqueray lived his own gospel in designs assigned to him: the palaces of Transportation, Horticulture and Agriculture. "The architect has subdued the use of sculpture in the building," he had explained to a reporter, before the exploitation censors could muzzle him. "He depends on mass effects and on the grouping of the masses. That is, he depends on architecture rather than on tawdry decorations for his effect."

Transportation was part of the Main Picture, so Masqueray permitted the merest decoration along its massed triple arches. But the Horticulture and Agriculture buildings, on the far western reach of the fairground, were not required to harmonize with the central theme, and they were simplicity itself. So was Cass Gilbert's Art Palace, the only permanent building on the fairground, sited at the crest of Art Hill. Gilbert, Taylor and Masqueray were trying to work out a scheme to screen the elegantly but incongruously chaste Art Palace with a temporary structure more in keeping with the rest of the Main Picture.

Masqueray's Palace of Transportation: a relatively simple design, based on contemporary French railway architecture. From The Universal Exposition of 1904. *Private collection.*

Louis had heard accounts of Gilbert's wrath back in June when the newspaper quoted Taylor as saying that "the Art Palace would not intrude its plainness on the pretty scene." Taylor had been forced to apologize, and claimed he was misquoted.

Though their collaboration had begun cordially enough, Taylor in St. Louis and Gilbert in New York were more and more at loggerheads because of terrible pressures of time and the crossing of telegrams in transit. Gilbert had been obliged to revise his work, significantly, several times. Masqueray's mediation was a help; still, Louis did not see a happy end to the relationship of Gilbert and the fair.

Feeling the November chill, Louis drew back from the window. Time to return to the architecture offices next door and his model of the Bienville Bridge. Leaving the administration building, Louis noted its Gothic details. Leased from Washington University for the duration of the fair, it would assume its intended purpose in 1905 as administrative headquarters of the new campus. The Division of Works occupied the second floor of another new building, immediately to the southwest, designed in the same style. There, in the stairwell, Louis was nearly knocked over by a draftsman racing to the hectograph machine in the basement. From the look of his blotched purple shirtsleeves, he had already spent a good deal of the morning down there, making copy after copy of plans for Masqueray's Transportation Palace. With shouts of laughter, another pair of draftsmen thundered along behind the first. Louis sprang from their path, smiling, reminded of the atelier.

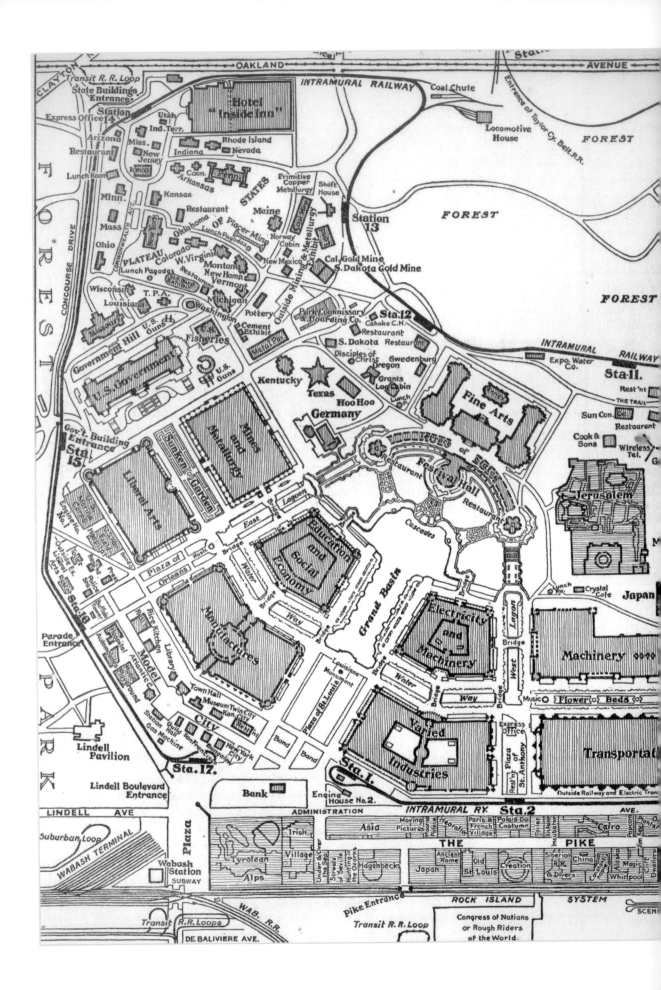

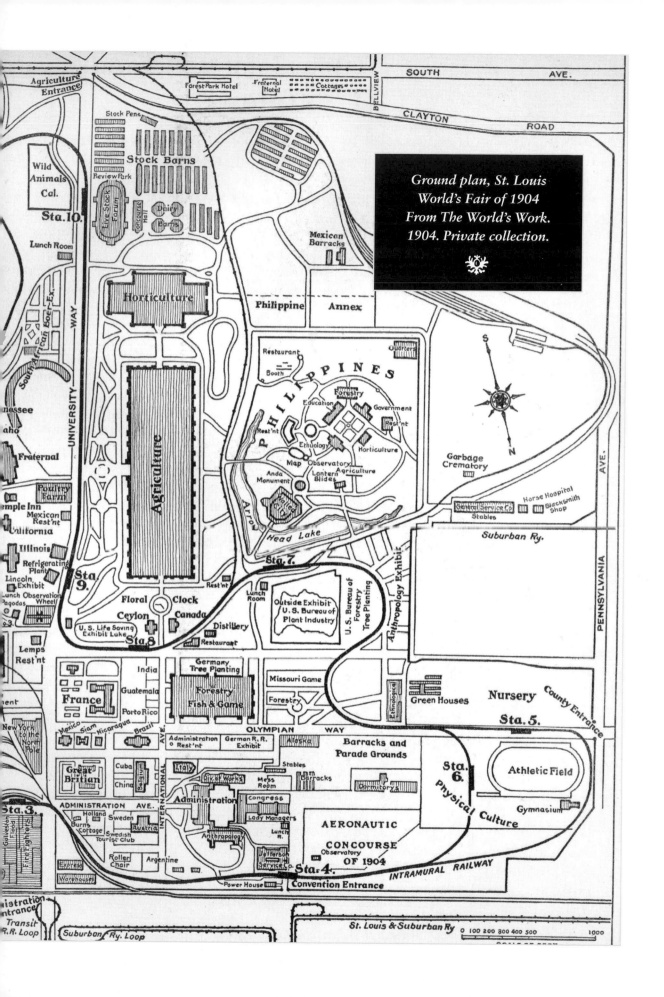

Ground plan, St. Louis
World's Fair of 1904
From The World's Work.
1904. Private collection.

Chapter Four

Making Magic

The Design Staff

"But it would take too long," recorded an observer, "to enumerate all the attractions of this remarkable exposition. Gondoliers from Venice piloted their gondolas through the canals and under the bridges....The grounds had been beautifully landscaped....Sculptors, painters, and architects had all contributed to enrich the scene. The scene was a dream world, full of song and silvery laughter."[1]

The writer was Louis LaBeaume (1873–1961), a St. Louis architect and World's Fair design staff colleague of Louis Spiering (FIG. 4.1). Scion of an old French family prominent in St. Louis, LaBeaume published his memoir in 1958, when he was 85. He had spent a lifetime cultivating the image of a patrician citizen-architect: he won important commissions (among them Kiel Auditorium and the Lindenwood College campus), acted as early proponent of the Jefferson National Expansion riverfront project, ruled the Saint Louis Art Museum during his ten years as chairman of the board of directors, and established himself as a witty belle-lettrist specializing in essays on architecture. His commentary seemed delivered from an ever-so-slightly elevated perspective, and that perspective was gimlet-eyed more often than not. If LaBeaume smiled, the camera never caught him at it. Yet forty-odd years after the exposition, he grew rhapsodic in remembrance. Such was the power of the St. Louis World's Fair of 1904.

Louis Spiering's memoir of the fair was entirely pictorial: a 68-page album of his snapshots and postcards,

FIG. 4.1 *Louisiana Purchase Exposition design staff at work in Busch Hall. Louis Spiering is seated, center, with coffee cup. Louis LaBeaume, with pipe, stands at Spiering's left. Spiering Album. MHS.*

which he titled "A History of the Louisiana Purchase Exposition." The album shows us Spiering's few independently designed buildings, as well as multitudes of decorative details on palaces and fairgrounds (FIG. 4.2 AND 4.3) created

FIG. 4.2 *The design staff created unifying details on the fairgrounds, such as the bridges crossing the lagoons. Above, the Daniel Boone Bridge, with Palace of Manufactures under construction in the background. Spiering Album. MHS*

FIG. 4.3 *Detail from bridge: a typical LPE lamp-post. Spiering Album. MHS.*

and orchestrated by the design department. Spiering appears to have intended the album only for his own later reference; an otherwise decent archivist in the documentation of his scrapbooks, he provided no captions.[2] But although Spiering's photographic memoir is wordless, it is far from mute. We can interpret the pictures in the context of Spiering's training, the architectural requirements of the exposition itself, and finally in the degree of interest Spiering took in certain buildings, as reflected by the number of times they appear.

Spiering, like LaBeaume, was vulnerable to the romance of the fair. He could not resist an occasional image of pure fancy—a construction shot of Art Hill that looks like the Acropolis; or that image captured by probably nearly every visitor who brought a camera to the fair: the magic of the palaces illuminated after dark, with thousands of lights reflecting in the lagoons below. Louis Spiering's awe was such that he did what any besotted tourist would do: in an act bordering on the elegiac, he made this ephemeral night scene the final image in his World's Fair photograph album.

The Mysterious Department of Design

Much of the exposition's fantasy was the work of Louis Spiering and his architect colleagues in the Department of Design. The department's occasional mention in the press in the early pre-fair years must have provoked curiosity, for Emmanuel Masqueray, chief of design, was called upon to explain. He did so in an essay circulated nationwide by the exposition publicity department:

FIG. 4.3

Masqueray began tongue in cheek:

"The function exercised by the Department of Design of the Louisiana Purchase Exposition is a puzzle to the average man interested in the construction of an exposition. It is a puzzle, however, that he is eager to solve to judge from the questions he asks. His principal difficulty is to find a field in which the Department of Design can work which is not covered by some other department. He knows that the commission of architects, headed by the Director of Works as chairman, plans the lay-out of the grounds. He knows that the Department of Civil Engineering writes this lay-out on the ground with stakes. He knows that the architects design the big buildings. He knows that the Landscape Department attends to the landscape, the electrical engineer to lighting, and the mechanical engineer to the water, and he cannot see that anything remains. He finally concludes, 'Ah, the Department of Design attends to the color of the buildings. That's it.'"[3]

Masqueray further explained that the design department was unique to American expositions, necessitated by the "magnificent distances" separating cities here. Because exposition architects live in far-flung corners, he said, it's too time-consuming to call them together to consult on every detail of the overall picture of the fair. "The Chief of Design," said Masqueray, "is therefore entrusted with studying and working out details which in foreign expositions are attended to by the architects in conference. He is, under the Director of Works, the resident representative of the commission of architects. This brings to the Department of Design the dressing up and decoration of the grounds, including the designing of all monumental, landscape and water effects. The Department of Design supplies the setting for the buildings of the

FIG. 4.4 *The design staff poses before a giant schematic drawing of the fairgrounds. Louis LaBeaume stands at far left. Louis Spiering is in the back row, behind a similarly white-smocked architect, probably Gustave Umbdenstock. Spiering Album. MHS.*

architects—the frame for their pictures. It designs the bridges and monuments, plans the treatment of the lagoons, the big water effects, the entrances, the gardens, the fountains, the lamp-posts and the music pavilions."[4]

Presumably this explanation hushed the clamor in 1902... at least it explained the "what." But a contemporary researcher who wants to determine the "who" of the design department is in for a merry chase (FIG. 4.4). Masqueray never names his staff. The financial records of the Louisiana Purchase Exposition Company are equally unhelpful; anyone on salary in an architectural capacity was classified as "draughtsman," from those at the bottom of the pay scale ($60 per month) to Louis Spiering, who at $195 per month was close to the top.[5]

In his memoir of the World's Fair, architect Louis LaBeaume gives us a few names: "They [the LPE Co.] had... organized a Department of Design under E. L. Masqueray, a Beaux Arts man....We had a pretty good group of draftsmen, including Frere Champney, Walter Karcher, George Nagle and Frank Swales."[6] These four young architects had been imported from firms on the East Coast, and at least two were in St. Louis at the express invitation of Masqueray. Nagle and Swales, in fact, had trained in Masqueray's New York *atelier*. The LPE press bureau announced their appointments when they were hired early in 1902; curiously, LaBeaume's name was not included in the news release, though he was hired at the same time and at a higher salary ($195 per month) than all but Champney. It is also odd that LaBeaume does not mention Spiering, who came on staff six months later; the two men worked side by side for more than a year, pursued similar architectural careers thereafter, were members of the same professional and civic organizations...and LaBeaume acted as honorary pallbearer in Spiering's funeral eight years after the fair.

In His Own Words

What did Louis Spiering actually do at the fair? Yearn as we might for a fully realized portrait of the Department of Design and all its activities, in the end we are left with something more akin to a police artist's sketch, a composite of a few facts and a great deal of subjective reminiscence. The facts of Spiering's World's Fair work, from an administrative standpoint, are found in LPE payroll records and a few news articles from the LPE press bureau that announce his appointment to the design staff and credit him with the design of the Palais du Costume, an attraction on the Pike. For everything else we must rely on Spiering's own accounts. This is not an uncomfortable stretch. A study of Spiering's career, one hundred years after the fact, finds him disinclined to hyperbole, or even self-promotion.[7]

Spiering's accounts of his World's Fair work are preserved in letters and career summaries sent post-1904 to prospective clients. In 1910, he wrote to Anna Sheldon that he had served as "First Assistant Designer of Louisiana Purchase Exposition, St. Louis, July, 1902–December 1903," and as

FIG. 4.5 *Early sketch of Art Hill, displayed by Spiering in his office. (See FIG. 5.8) MHS.*

"Consulting and supervising architect for French and Austrian Governments" at the fair.[8] In another career summary, he stated that he was responsible for several small exposition buildings: the Palais du Costume, the Wireless Telegraph Tower and the Express Office (FIG. 4.5).

Trouble in Paradise

Architecture is a profession in which creative authorship sometimes blurs. But just because this is understood does not mean it is tacitly accepted. Louis LaBeaume's memoir of the design staff hints at conflict, echoing the disputes that occasionally flared between uber-director Isaac Taylor and the principal architects. LaBeaume paints an unflattering and surprisingly personal picture of design chief Emmanuel Masqueray, his superior. Dropping his characteristic air of detachment, LaBeaume says: "Masqueray was a vain little man about five-foot-

FIG. 4.6 *Emmanuel Masqueray (hatted, gesticulating figure at center of group) on site with his staff during early planning stages of the fair. Spiering Album. MHS.*

four, with a sandy complexion and a pointed beard. He wasn't really any vainer than a good many architects that we all have known, but he was conscious of his abilities. He was a bachelor and brought his mother out to live with him. We never knew his exact age, but he said to me, 'LaBeaume, I am blonde so I don't grow gray.' His mother had a birthday and we all chipped in and sent her a huge bunch of roses. The next morning he appeared in the office all smiles. 'Fellows,' he said, 'Mama was so happy with those roses. You could not have made her more happy if you had sent her a folding bed studded with diamonds.'"[9]

LaBeaume then recalls his fellow designer Francis Swales. "He was a very clever draftsman, and would work late revising and improving the 'master's' designs. Naturally a good deal of time was wasted this way, because we always went back to the master."[10]

One wonders if there might have been animosity between LaBeaume and Masqueray (FIG. 4.6). If so, it could have had something to do with a bold move by LaBeaume: his extremely early execution of a World's Fair design. On June 29, 1901, the *St. Louis Globe-Democrat* published an architectural drawing of a $100,000 building to be erected at the fair by the Travelers' Protective Association of America, a St. Louis-based advocacy organization for commercial travelers. An accompanying cutline noted that the architect was Louis A. LaBeaume.

Revisited in 2003, the timing of this news release appears to be an act of colossal cheek, on the part of either LaBeaume or the TPA, or both: it was published more than a week before the announcement of names of the principal fair architects—let alone their palace designs, or rules for general design standards for auxiliary buildings. Of course the TPA may have been responsible—what a coup, after all, to be the first organization to step forward as a fair participant, and with a handsome building already designed! And by a native son who happened to be the son of the organization's national secretary/treasurer! But even in 1901, the gesture may well have seemed a frank statement of entitlement by LaBeaume, a Napoleonic declaration of himself as a World's Fair architect. It does not seem a gesture calculated to please when it reached the ears of Emmanuel Masqueray, LaBeaume's eventual superior, whose name does not appear in the LPE Executive Committee minutes as design chief candidate for another month. It may be no coincidence that while LaBeaume appears to have joined the design staff (though whether at Masqueray's invitation is unrecorded), that fact was not marked by the same administrative acknowledgment that heralded the appointments of Champney, Karcher, Nagle, Swales and Spiering.

As for the TPA building, LaBeaume does not mention it in his World's Fair reminiscence. It did get built, but the original design was altered until it bore no more resemblance to the reality than a flamingo to a duck. [See Chapter Seven.]

Playing Politics

If there is a political reason for the absence of LaBeaume's name from announcements of World's Fair design staff appointments, might there be a corresponding reason for the almost fawning portrayal of another young architect of about the same modest accomplishments? There is if we focus our investigation on the *World's Fair Bulletin*, house organ of the Louisiana Purchase Exposition Company.

The *Bulletin* was a monthly tabloid, resplendent with full-page photographs of dignitaries, exposition palaces and the like. Its titular editor/proprietor was former newspaperman Colin Selph, though David R. Francis himself told a correspondent: "The Exposition management edits the matter

which goes on the first 15 pages."[11] The *Bulletin*, as might
be expected, was wildly subjective. In February 1904, it paid
sudden editorial homage to Charles Deitering, a contemporary
of Louis Spiering, with a photograph and the following
message: "In our generation we have architects who have never
been excelled in their sphere of endeavor—men like Charles
H. Deitering, of St. Louis, who, though a comparatively young
man, has made a national fame in his profession, and whose
achievements in the past forespeak for him a pre-eminent place
in the annals of American architecture."[12]

Charles Deitering was assuredly an architect of respectable
accomplishment (and went on to an equally respectable though
hardly remarkable career, lacking the eventual distinction
of, say, Louis LaBeaume's). He was a graduate of MIT and
an assistant in the private practice of Isaac Taylor. Perhaps
because of this connection, Deitering was named supervising
architect for the Chinese and Brazilian pavilions on the
fairgrounds. But what, one wonders, prompted the kind of
editorial effulgence the *Bulletin* usually reserved for the star
architects of the principal palaces?

A possible answer is found in the previous month's minutes
of the LPE Executive Committee. On January 19, 1904, the
committee learned of an offer that Deitering had made to
Isaac Taylor, proposing to "erect sixteen stations [on the
fairground's] Intramural Railroad at his own cost according to
Exposition plans, and [to] pay 15% on the gross receipts from
the sale of lunches and beverages in said stations."[13] Of this
handsome offer—the missing news hook—the *Bulletin* article
says nothing.

Realities

Deitering, through his employment with Isaac Taylor, had
a connection to the "Big Cinch," that powerful group of St.
Louis leaders with interlocking business and social alliances.
They ran the city, and by extension, the fair. Not surprisingly,
Deitering was awarded exposition work, responded in kind,
and was publicly anointed in the *World's Fair Bulletin*.

LaBeaume could have expected preferential treatment as
well. Educated at Columbia University, and very briefly at the
Ecole des Beaux-Arts, he had found enviable employment in
Boston with the architectural firm Peabody and Stearns. He

had social connections to the Big Cinch—at one point, whether he knew it or not, he even had members of the prominent Skinker family lobbying David R. Francis for his appointment to the fair architectural staff.[14] But for some reason, LaBeaume got short shrift in the *World's Fair Bulletin*, which should have been one of his stoutest boosters.

Spiering had two significant connections, but neither one linked him to the Big Cinch. Though the Bernays and Spiering families held a respected position in St. Louis, they were allied with the artistic, intellectual and liberal German sectors of the upper middle class, rather than the elite of Vandeventer Place cum Central West End. Louis Spiering came to his World's Fair employment almost assuredly through his architectural pedigree—the imprimatur of the Ecole.

Thus employed, Spiering held another trump: Thekla Bernays, the "Aunt Thekla" of his boyhood on Chambers Street. Everybody was aware of Miss Bernays. A walking cauldron of intellectual ferment, Aunt Thekla had been one of the earliest members of the St. Louis Artists' Guild, the Ethical Society of St. Louis and a founding member of the prestigious Wednesday Club for women. Fluent in five languages, she had translated several libretti as well as "a very abstruse subject in metaphysics."[15] Thekla Bernays made regular trips to Europe; these generated reports so engaging that she became a contributor to the *St. Louis Globe-Democrat*. She was the great good friend of St. Louisan William Marion Reedy, editor of the nationally known literary weekly, the *Mirror*, to which she also became a contributor.

By 1902, Thekla Bernays knew her way around the printed page, and the journalistic forces that set the presses in motion. Admittedly she was not in a position to influence either the World's Fair publicity machine or the *St. Louis Republic*, both controlled by David R. Francis. But she knew the people at the *Globe*. And that may be the reason that the *Globe*, after running a lackluster announcement of Spiering's addition to the design staff, came back ten days later with a considerably more detailed account of the young St. Louis architect. "LOUIS C. SPIERING," read the headline, "A St. Louisan Who Has Distinguished Himself in Architecture."[16] This version was accompanied by a handsome, two-column portrait photograph.

Stated the conclusion: "He is eminently equipped for his position, having witnessed at closest range the last two universal expositions, the Columbian of 1893 and the Paris exposition of 1900, with eye and mind specially trained to observe architectural features (FIG. 4.7 AND 4.8). In view of this fact, the addition of Mr. Spiering to the Masqueray staff is a singularly happy one."

FIG. 4.7 AND FIG. 4.8 *Spiering recorded before-and-after versions of construction on Art Hill. To the left is Festival Hall. The arc continues with the Colonnade of States, terminating in the West Restaurant Pavilion. Spiering Album. MHS.*

In the long run, publicity was of scant importance to members of the St. Louis design staff. Working on this fair was not the career-maker the young architects might have wished. None of the names we associate with the design staff ever achieved the status of an Eames or a Link, locally, or of Stanford White, John Carrere or Cass Gilbert. LaBeaume and Spiering remained in St. Louis to make their mark on their native city, where much still is owed to both men. Walter Thompson Karcher enjoyed a solid, long-term career in Philadelphia. Edouard Frere Champney migrated eventually to the West Coast, establishing a practice in Seattle. Francis Swales designed in London and Vancouver and wrote often in architectural journals. George Nagle eludes us, as do any other bona fide designers unnamed in LaBeaume's memoir.

PHOTOGRAPHS

A compendium of rarely seen photographs from the personal album of Louis Spiering

All photographs from the Spiering Album, Missouri Historical Society, St. Louis, with special thanks to Duane R. Sneddeker

Opposite: Louis Spiering (left) and unidentified friend meeting at the fair.

Pre-fair views. Far upper left: rows of stands for castings. Center, a steam tractor pulls a grading machine, while below, a Marion steam shovel is being set up. Clockwise from above left: waterways under construction; the artistry inherent in structure and shadow; and snow-shrouded fairgrounds-in-the-making.

Architectural details were the
subtle unifiers of the fairgrounds.
Spiering was interested in features
of Emmanuel Masqueray's Palace
of Transportation: the turrets
(opposite upper left) that repeated
his Louisiana Purchase Monument
nearby; as well as other sculptural
elements of the Palace facade
(opposite upper right and right).
Pentagonal flag standards (opposite
below) and graceful bridges
crossing lagoons (above) were
additional repeating motifs.

The Washington State Building (above left), located on the Plateau of States, was a unique wooden wigwam that spotlighted Washington's lumber industry. Spiering captured this example of vernacular architecture, as well as the Mission-style Lifesaving Exhibit. The latter may have inspired his later interest in the University Methodist Church in Austin, Texas. (FIG. 10.11)

Spiering's talent in modelage was called upon in the design of this ram's head urn, which he shot in close-up (opposite, with unidentified woman) and in context of its placement on the Colonnade of States (above).

Spiering's amateur camera was barely up to the challenges of indoor photography. Still, he tried to record his sculptural entrance to the Cuauhtemoc Brewery exhibit (above, opposite), displayed by the Mexican brewer in the Palace of Agriculture. Fashioned of wood and staff, the semicircular entry represented a portion of a barrel, and was richly decorated in a motif of hops leaves intertwined through a trellis. A statue of Mexican hero Cuauhtemoc, symbol of the brewery, crowned the entry.

Opposite: Two sculptures that eventually flanked the monumental "Spirit of the Atlantic" by Isidore Konti. Spiering caught them waiting in the wings for installation outside the West Restaurant Pavilion just above the West Cascades.

"Creation" (above left), a concession on the Pike, was situated directly across from Spiering's Palais du Costume. It was probably the only example of French art nouveau architecture on the fairgrounds.

Festival Hall (above right) contained the world's largest pipe organ within the world's largest dome, and seating for 3,500. But visitors there suffered from inferior acoustics until the problem was corrected. Perhaps that was the reason Spiering wanted to record this view of the interior.

Spiering balanced his detail shots with panoramic views of the fairgrounds by night (left) and by day. Above, the Palace of Liberal Arts, and to its rear, the United States Government Building. Below, southeast view from the roof of Festival Hall.

Chapter Five

"A Magnificent View"

The West Restaurant Pavilion

The West Restaurant Pavilion was part of the diadem that crowned the fair (FIG. 5.1). At the apex of this arc was the exuberant Festival Hall, whose dome was the largest in the world. A colonnade extended from either side of Festival Hall, each wing terminating in a circular pavilion. All three buildings in this Cascade crescent overlooked the splendid falls that tumbled down Art Hill and splashed into the Grand Basin. But the restaurant pavilions were planned to offer the best view.

FIG. 5.1 *The West Restaurant Pavilion. Grillework in the dome was highlighted in gold. Spiering Album. MHS.*

As Emmanuel Masqueray described it: "Here the Exposition visitors can get one of the most magnificent views that the earth holds out. In front of the visitor three gigantic cascades, the largest artificial falls of water on earth, will, by successive leaps that churn its limpid flow to foamy white, plunge into a vast basin that stretches far away between the white colonnade buildings and the magnificent avenues of giant maples, planted and pruned with military precision, and sheltering, with their green, scores of white statues....Here will be gardens with flowers and shrubs and trees, lawns of close-clipped blue grass, vases, fountains and statuary, white stairs and stone walks and frames of low stone balustrades....The picture will never be forgotten by those who see it, and never will they want to forget it."[1]

This beautiful scene, which would become emblematic of the 1904 World's Fair, took full advantage of Forest Park's unique attributes: hills and terraces. Though prior

FIG. 5.2 *Cass Gilbert.*
From World's Fair
Bulletin. *St. Louis*
Public Library.

expositions had featured dramatic water effects and lushly planted walkways, they had been laid out on flat terrain. The LPE architectural commission quickly arrived at a striking alternative, a design that they likened to an open fan. With Festival Hall at the fan's focal point, the principal exhibition palaces radiated downhill to the north along five axes.

Cass Gilbert (1859–1934), the famous New York architect, was to play a principal role in the creation of the Main Picture. Gilbert, age 42 at the time of his appointment to the commission of architects, had worked for McKim, Mead and White early in his career, and was later a partner of James Knox Taylor. Gilbert had already designed the Minnesota State Capitol and the United States Custom House in New York.[2]

Gilbert's Festival Hall was the center of attention on Art Hill. In fact, it served a dual purpose as focal point and also as a screen for the building behind it: a considerably more restrained Art Palace, also assigned to Gilbert, which was planned as the only permanent exhibition building on the fairgrounds (FIG. 5.3 AND 5.4). Gilbert's relationship with Isaac

FIG. 5.3

Taylor soured fairly early in the course of this collaboration. Gilbert is sometimes characterized as temperamental. In 1904 he resigned from the LPE architectural commission, and sued the LPE Company for $47,113.04. Because of miscommunications with Taylor, changes imposed by several administrative committees, and revised concepts of the Main Picture, Gilbert would be required to redesign his Art Palace/Festival Hall complex nearly half a dozen times. "[Committee members] tried to move his building off the hill site planned for it; they threatened to take it away from him entirely; they eventually decided to screen it from the Main Picture of the Fair (allowing him to design the screening building); and finally refused to pay him for his second building."[3] The case went to trial in 1905, and Gilbert was ultimately paid $6,454.60.

With Masqueray, however, Gilbert was far more simpatico. Gilbert designed the exterior of Festival Hall; Masqueray was given charge of decorating the interior. The two men did disagree on one of the most arresting features

FIG. 5.3 AND FIG. 5.4 *Gilbert's Palace of Art (left), at the crest of Art Hill, was a restrained design befitting a permanent installation. It was shielded from view by his exuberant Festival Hall (above). Photographs from* The Greatest of Expositions. *Private collection.*

*Viewed three-dimensionally (*FIG. *5.5,* above) *or aerially* (FIG. *5.6), the Art Hill arc was the fair's dominant feature. Drawings from* World's Fair Bulletin, *St. Louis Public Library; and* The World's Work, *Private collection. Even Masqueray's imposing Louisiana Purchase Monument (*FIG. *5.7) stood in obeisance. From* The Universal Exposition of 1904. *Private collection.*

of the Main Picture. Masqueray was assigned responsibility for the colonnades and restaurant pavilions (though these features were adapted from Gilbert's original design of the Art Palace complex). Where would Gilbert's work leave off and Masqueray's begin? Gilbert suggested that Masqueray take over the exterior design of Festival Hall at the level of the main floor. Gilbert made the offer, writes architectural historian Pamela Hemenway Simpson, even though he knew that Masqueray wanted the main cascade to begin directly in front of and level with the entrance to Festival Hall. Gilbert took exception: "I think it is not 'good architecture' to have a great mass of water...gush from the facade of the building," he wrote. But Masqueray stuck to his plan, and the hall gushed.[4]

It is interesting that a team so heavily populated with bachelors—a fact gleefully noted by the *Globe-Democrat,* singling out Taylor, Masqueray, and nearly half a dozen others[5]—should have labored in service to a ground plan so essentially feminine in concept. The architects described the layout as fan-shaped, but to a contemporary eye perhaps more attuned to anatomical drawings studied in preparation for Lamaze classes, the aerial view appears less fanlike than fallopian. Observed

three-dimensionally, the crowning scene on Art
Hill is a 1,200-foot encirclement, the ultimate
Mother-Earth embrace. Quite a different symbol
had dominated the 1901 exposition in Buffalo:
the "phallic implications" of its Electric Tower
are critically noted a century later.[6] But in 1904
St. Louis, even Masqueray's shaftlike Louisiana
Purchase Monument (a motif repeated on the
corner towers atop his Transportation building)
is of lesser import, standing in tribute to the
panoramic arc opposite and above the Cascades
(FIG. 5.5–5.7).

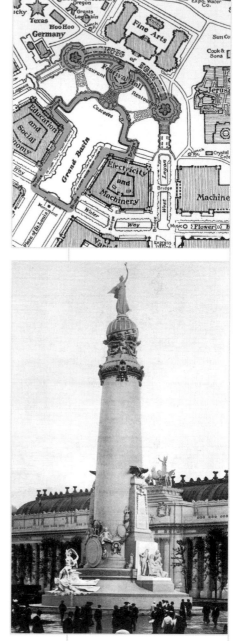

Masqueray had designed an elaborate closing
to the central axes, a short distance to the north
of the Louisiana Purchase Monument, a highly
decorative screen that would make the northern
horizon of the fairground as lovely to the observer
at the Cascades as the Cascades were to the
visitor looking south from the Louisiana Purchase
Monument. By 1904, this plan was officially
scrapped because of lack of time as well as funds.
So the three principal axes terminated, according
to local critic Frederick Mann, in "the ragged
outline" of scenery on the Pike, a "hideous blue
dome" (the "Creation" concession on the Pike)
and "a structural steel tower with no elements
either of beauty or fitness to the place." He was
referring to the American De Forest Wireless
Telegraph Tower, about which much will be
said in Chapter Nine. Mann offered similar
criticism of the fairgrounds as a whole. His essay,
"Architecture at the Exposition," published in the
Bulletin of the Washington University Association,
was a fair and non-elitist commentary in spite
of Mann's authoritative position as chairman of
the architecture program at the university (and as such, Louis

FIG. 5.6 (*above*) AND 5.7

Spiering's faculty superior). However, his opinions could not
have won him civic favor or sympathy from the local architects
he so unstintingly criticized. An Ecole *ancien* and 1902 import
from Philadelphia, Mann left Washington University in 1910.[7]

Whose Design?

While the many permutations of the Art Palace/Festival Hall complex were being worked out, Masqueray pressed on with plans for the twin restaurant pavilions. The December 1902 issue of the *World's Fair Bulletin* published Masqueray's handsome rendering of the restaurant pavilion facade. Or was it Masqueray's rendering? By December, Louis Spiering had been on the job for four months. Could the master have entrusted him with the design of the pavilion?

Louis Spiering's role in the West Restaurant Pavilion is more ambiguous than in any other exposition building with which he was associated. In fact, he never claimed authorship. However, his scrapbook and photo album show intensely focused interest in this structure. And at least twice in reliable sources, he was credited with the design.

In 1905, examples of Spiering's designs were shown in an exhibit of St. Louis artists' work. The accompanying catalog text written by well-known sculptor George Julian Zolnay stated that Spiering had been "Assistant Chief of Design at the Louisiana Purchase Exposition, and as such designed the Restaurant Pavilions and Colonnades on Art Hill, the Horticulture Building, Bridges, etc."[8]

Seven years later, Spiering's obituary in the *St. Louis Republic* stated: "Mr. Spiering designed...the pavilion on either side of the Cascades at the St. Louis World's Fair."

Also worth noting are the many pavilion views in Spiering's photo album, as well as the presence of the pavilion in a photograph of Spiering in 1904 (FIG. 5.8). It shows him seated in his architectural office in the Chemical Building. Mounted on the wall behind him are an early schematic drawing of the Main Picture, his rendering of the Palais du Costume and photograph of a restaurant pavilion.

If Spiering actually designed the restaurant pavilions, why didn't he say so? Possibly as a mark of respect, in the *eleve/patron* tradition of the Ecole des Beaux-Arts. Masqueray, after all, had publicly received the credit. It would not have done for the master's assistant to claim authorship. But outsiders such as Zolnay or family members contributing information for an obituary, with no allegiance to Ecole traditions and full awareness of fact, may have felt no compunctions about calling a designer a designer.

Pavilion as Flash Point

As opening day drew nearer, observant visitors to the fairgrounds understood the importance of a design department: the Main Picture was taking on a pleasing unity, thanks to Masqueray's repeating visual themes. One of the most prominent was the pentagonal motif that appeared in flag standards placed throughout the Main Picture. They were smaller repetitions of the imposing restaurant pavilions, designed as pentagons, explained Masqueray, to harmonize with the five axes radiating from Festival Hall.[9]

By early 1904, a guidebook writer described the pavilion architecture as "a spherical pentagon, the five faces projecting in beautiful curves. The colonnade is of the French Ionic order, supporting a richly decorated entablature that carries an open balustrade. Between these architectural motifs are massive pylons that serve as bases for decorative flagpoles. One of the most novel features in the construction of these pavilions is that of the balustrade surrounding the terrace, from which rises the drum wall. This in turn serves as a base for the dome. This dome is encircled by a richly ornamental belt, and the sides are panels of open-work that lend lightness and airiness to the general effect."[10]

Public enthusiasm for the hilltop restaurant aeries already had been whetted by Masqueray's promise of a vantage point that would treat visitors to "one of the most magnificent views the earth holds out." Could Masqueray—or anyone—have known that the Louisiana Purchase Exposition Company Executive Committee had designs on one of these choice locations?

FIG. 5.8 *Louis Spiering in his architectural office, June 1904. Photograph courtesy of The Sheldon Art Galleries.*

On March 7, 1904, the story broke: "AN EXCLUSIVE CLUB FOR THE FAIR—To Occupy West Pavilion" read the headline in the *St. Louis Globe-Democrat*. It described the efforts of the Louisiana Purchase Exposition Company Entertainment Committee to secure the West Restaurant Pavilion for an "exclusive club" that would serve as entertainment headquarters for fair officers and their guests. "It is one of the nicest locations on the grounds," noted the *Globe*. "The pavilion on the east end of the terrace will be occupied by Mrs. Rohrer [sic], the famous authority on things to eat. While the East pavilion will be the home of scientific and simple cooking, the West one may be turned over to the club for eight-course dinners."[11]

The appropriation of the west pavilion actually had been in the works for several months. The topic makes its first brief appearance in the December 7, 1902, meeting minutes of the LPE Company executive committee, with action deferred.[12] By the January 21 meeting, plans were underway: "The President laid before the Committee the proposed plan of the club to take and conduct West Pavilion Restaurant." Appointed to study the matter, a special subcommittee submitted its recommendations on April 9. First, they recommended that the "Fair City Club plan [the first appearance of its name in the minutes, with no mention of particulars] be abandoned."[13] They submitted two alternatives, and on April 12, the executive committee adopted the following:

1. The Directors of the Exposition to pay into a fund to be used for furnishing the Pavilion the sum of $9,000, or the sum of $100 each.

2. Twenty-five percent of the gross receipts from the conduct of the Pavilion to be paid to the Exposition Company.

3. A rental of $7,000 to be paid to the Exposition Company.

4. The two upper floors of the Pavilion to be reserved for the uses of the Exposition Company and as it may deem proper and service to be given there from the restaurant on the ground floor.[14]

The following day, the *St. Louis Globe-Democrat* reacted: "The proposed Fair City club, in its original form, failed of approval by the directors, and the proposition was given a new shuffle, so that the directors will have a club in the west pavilion restaurant on Art Hill without it being called a club."[15]

Five days later, the LPE grounds and buildings committee approved a $1,145 bid by the firm Strehlow & Phelps to add two "shower baths" in the basement of the west pavilion, to enhance the service area of the second story and to install a new floor on the third-story balcony.[16] Moving quickly, for opening day of the fair was just one week away, the executive committee recast its exploratory subcommittee as the West Pavilion Supply Committee, and authorized this body to "expend for furniture and supplies the sum of $15,000."[17]

An important administrative detail remained. The defunct Fair City Club had appeared to be so sure a thing that a club manager had been hired, who now was owed back pay. In a letter that appears to lean on David R. Francis to honor this commitment, committee member Francis D. Hirschberg points out that one Gus Koenig had left his job with the Pullman Company in another city for employment at the LPE, to "perfect arrangements and take charge of what would have been The Fair City Club, his compensation to be $250 per month salary and 15% of the net profits." Hirschberg recommends a payment of $500 for services rendered. The payment was authorized.[18]

In his exhaustive report on the fair, written a decade later, Francis addresses the matter of the club: "A Directors' club was maintained in the West Pavilion on the World's Fair grounds. The membership was limited to the Directors of the Exposition, foreign and state commissioners and visitors, including their wives and families. This club not only admirably supplied the facilities for official entertaining, but also furnished a meeting place where those actively engaged in managing the affairs of the great Exposition could exchange ideas and develop and promote a closer feeling of cordiality and mutual interest. The advantages of this club were well attested by its popularity, and by the further fact that it was the scene of every important entertainment that the size of the structure would permit. It was the recognized policy of the exposition management to confine entertainments and other official functions to the World's Fair Grounds. Under this policy the West Pavilion had an important part in the social life of the Exposition."[19]

Chapter Six

Old and New

The French and Austrian Pavilions

I n the years following the fair, Louis Spiering was continually updating the project list he submitted to prospective clients. He added new projects, while deleting some of the older commissions. He might mention some or most of his World's Fair projects. But the one World's Fair assignment he never failed to mention was that of supervising architect, a position he filled for both French and Austrian governments erecting pavilions in St. Louis.

The buildings could not have differed more dramatically. France had chosen a historic icon as its symbol at the St. Louis World's Fair of 1904: a meticulously reproduced Grand Trianon (Fig. 6.1), the seventeenth-century Versailles retreat built by Louis XIV for his mistress, Madame de Maintenon. Austria, in contrast, would startle American fairgoers with its avant-garde Secessionist architecture.

France was the first of the two nations to commit; by summer of 1902, the French commissioner to the fair was completing preliminary plans to reproduce the Petit Trianon, a smaller Versailles installation, on the fifteen-acre (Fig. 6.2) site at the southwest corner of University Boulevard and Olympian Way (now Skinker and Forsyth boulevards). Grading of the site had already begun, when France, at the beginning of January 1903, announced a change: the Petit Trianon was to be replaced by the more imposing Grand Trianon. "It is believed," speculated the *Globe-Democrat*, that "the change was prompted by Germany's intention to construct a castle like those on the cliffs along the Rhine."[1] Germany did reproduce the Charlottenburg Palace on a prominent fairgrounds site

Fig. 6.1 *Gustave Umbdenstock, architect of the French Pavilion, stands at the entry to pavilion grounds. Spiering Album. MHS.*

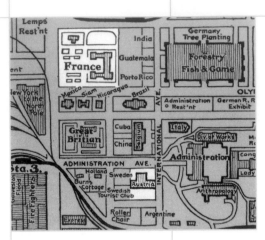

Fɪɢ. 6.2 *Map detail, western section of fairgrounds. The French Pavilion is top left; the Austrian Pavilion is lower center. Private collection.*

Fɪɢ. 6.3 *Calling card of Marcel Lambert. Private collection.*

between the Mines and Metallurgy building and the East Restaurant Pavilion.

The participation of foreign nations was important to exposition organizers; the greater the variety and quality of exhibitors, the more visitors the fair would attract. Forty-three nations erected pavilions at the St. Louis World's Fair of 1904,[2] used not only for display of technological advances and native arts and crafts, but also for diplomatic receptions and social occasions. At the stone and pink marble replica of the Grand Trianon, highly placed officials of the French government could lavishly entertain dignitaries from all over the world.

France shone some of her brightest architectural lights on this exhibition. Gustave Umbdenstock and Roger Bouvard of the Ecole were jointly named architect. Jules Vacherot, who had served as landscape designer for the 1900 Exposition Universelle in Paris, was commissioned to create the extensive gardens surrounding the French Pavilion. Interior exhibits at the pavilion, coordinated by Andre Vincent, included French treasures such as Gobelin tapestries and Sevres china. (Most of the nation's fine art exhibit was displayed nearby in the Art Palace, where Vincent oversaw its installation.)

All of the French architects dedicated long periods of weeks and even months to their respective assignments in St. Louis. But none could be on site for the approximately seventeen-month stretch from final agreement on an exhibit plan to its inaugural celebration in mid-April 1904. And that is probably where Louis Spiering came in.

The Commission

In January 1903, Spiering received a short note scribbled on Marcel Lambert's calling card (Fɪɢ. 6.3). In French, the patron greeted Spiering and informed him that "Bouvard fils" was inclined to consider him for the work going on at the St. Louis exposition. "I must write to you," he added.[3]

Lambert's message may have been part of a chain of events triggered a month earlier. France had entered into a

contract assigning all details of erecting the French Pavilion to a St. Louis agent of the American Express Company. On December 20, 1902, the *St. Louis Globe-Democrat* reported: "The express company has already invited from architects and contractors bids and plans for the French building and has transmitted them to the government." It is likely that Spiering responded to the call and placed his name before the decision makers in France.

Spiering's credentials made him a worthy candidate. His Beaux-Arts diploma assured the chief architects that he would be in sympathy not only with the project, but also with the intentions of his superiors. And his fluency in French meant that he could communicate effectively in his daily encounters with the nearly three hundred French laborers dispatched to St. Louis to work on the compound (FIG. 6.4).

It is easy to imagine Spiering, so recently graduated from the Ecole, welcoming the French architectural luminaries to his native city. They may have been in the assemblage at Ledoyen's on that night in Paris not so long ago, when Spiering, the new *diplomé*, was toasted with champagne. Now he was routinely in contact with the senior architects. Perhaps he even called on them at 3629 Lindell Boulevard—the residence leased by the French government for French commissioner Michel Lagrave and visiting dignitaries. Certainly they would have been welcome in his own home nearby at 3928 Lindell Boulevard. In early 1904, Spiering, now instructor of architecture at Washington University, escorted Gustave Umbdenstock to the

FIG. 6.4 *The French Pavilion, a replica of the Grand Trianon. From* The Greatest of Expositions. *Private collection.*

architectural department. There the eminent architect and *atelier patron* met students and critiqued their work.[4]

French Sensibilities

Landscape gardener Jules Vacherot was unimpressed with the St. Louis exposition as it stood at the end of 1903. Upon his return to Paris after work on the fairgrounds, he stated that the French pavilion "and two others which follow French designs are the only structures in the Exposition that do not strike horror into the delicate soul of a Parisian," reported the *St. Louis Globe-Democrat*. "'Everything has been sacrificed to ornate exteriors,' he declares." And: "'In their buildings at the St. Louis Fair the Americans have tried to imitate the French, but without artistic taste. Lacking in that, they are rearing extraordinary architectural anomalies. They have only succeeded in coarsely caricaturing their model, the Paris exposition of 1900.'"[5]

Umbdenstock, arriving in St. Louis two months later for his inspection of the nearly completed pavilion, was left to mend fences. "O no, it is not like the Paris exposition," he told a *Globe-Democrat* reporter, sketching as he spoke. "The buildings are imposing, magnificent. The architecture? It is beautiful in its simplicity. Simplicity is the keynote to successful art; the expression of the highest form of art. I was delighted to find the purity of style represented in the buildings. I admire especially the style represented in the Agriculture, Transportation and the Forestry buildings."[6] Diplomatically, he did not remind the reporter that all three were designed by Masqueray.

In Louis Spiering's photograph album, the French Pavilion is curiously underrepresented. One of only three images is a postcard picture of the Garden of the Trianon. The second shows a front view of the Trianon and grounds, centered behind one of the large and exquisite wrought iron gates at the opening of the long iron fence marking the entire perimeter of the pavilion. In front of the gate stands Gustave Umbdenstock, his face obscured in deep shadow. Finally, an out-of-focus close-up captures the wrought iron ornament on an exterior wall of the Trianon. It may be that of all the features of the pavilion, its decorative ironwork was of greatest interest to Louis Spiering.

Austria

As sensitive as St. Louisans were to French opinion, as eagerly as they bowed to French ideals of style, whether traditional or contemporary, they looked askance at new ideas coming from Austria and Germany. A lengthy photo feature story of the day on "Phases

FIG. 6.5 *Austrian Pavilion. From* **The Greatest of Expositions.** *Private collection.*

of the Dress Reform Movement" pointed out in its subhead the "gracefulness of the French" and the "ugliness of the German."[7] This fashion writer deplored the unstructured, corsetless style coming into vogue with her Teutonic sisters. No one could deny that a most unusual, disturbing aesthetic was drifting westward from the Rhine. And that was never more clearly manifested than in the facade of a latecomer to the exposition's line-up of foreign displays: the Austrian Pavilion.

To the eyes of the American public, the Austrian pavilion was one of the most peculiar structures on the fairgrounds (FIG. 6.5). Even the *World's Fair Bulletin*, in a rare burst of candor, had to admit: "Its exterior, which is in the 'art nouveau' style, is not appreciated by all the visitors, because of their being more familiar with the classical architecture which is seen in most of the buildings of the Fair."[8] But, added the *Bulletin*: "The facades of the Austrian Pavilion are admired by critics." Louis Spiering was evidently one who "got it," because he made it the runner-up for the single most photographed structure of his oeuvre. In a series of eleven shots, Spiering captured the front and side elevations and the gardens, and attempted one of the interior, focusing (not so successfully) on a couple posing before the entrance to a gallery.

Lines and Curves

The exterior was not actually "the art nouveau style" marked by whiplash curves and forms from nature, seen

FIG. 6.6 *Proposed West Pine entry (not built) to Forest Park, 2001, which was never built. Image courtesy of the office of Lawrence Halprin.*

FIG. 6.7 *Palace of Mines and Metallurgy, Theodore Link, architect. From* The Universal Exposition of 1904. *Private collection.*

elsewhere on the fairgrounds in the illustrations of Mucha, the jewelry of Lalique and the art glass of Tiffany. Art nouveau, having come into its own at the 1900 Paris exposition, was a phenomenon with powers to repel and attract simultaneously. The public was divided then, as now. (Witness St. Louisans' negative reactions in 2001 to Lawrence Halprin's designs (FIG. 6.6) for nouveau-reminiscent decorative gates at Forest Park.) Many people felt as Professor James Pattison, an arts writer and instructor, who addressed the members of St. Louis' Wednesday Club in 1903. "The speaker," said a reporter, "touched upon the idea of the moral influence of lines and curves, and assented that too much Art Nouveau was distinctly cloying, and that a 'Revolt' became revolting unless handled by an artist of refinement and quiet reserve."[9] Probably the LPE's only architectural example of this strain of art nouveau occurred on the Pike. (See Chapter Eight.)

In 1901, St. Louis architect Theodore Link unveiled plans for his contribution to the exposition, the clearly Viennese-inspired edifice that eventually became the Palace of Mines and Metallurgy (FIG. 6.7). Anticipating public censure, he sought to enlighten: "Let us…name it 'Secession Architecture.' Perhaps I will have to explain what [that] is, if the name should not make it quite clear. It means architectural liberty and emancipation with a strong plea for individuality. It is a breaking away from conventionality in design; it is more an architecture of feeling than of formula."[10]

The curveless Austrian pavilion was a pure example of Secessionist architecture, an allied form of art nouveau, characterized by severe rectilinear forms and subdued ornamentation. Secessionism had arisen a decade earlier in Munich, and then in Vienna, where one of its chief proponents, architect Joseph Maria Olbrich, designed a revolutionary exhibition hall (1897–1898) in which progressive artists could show their work. Called the Secession Exhibition Building, it was also known as "the Golden Cabbage" because of its proximity to the city's vegetable market and its principal ornamentation: a dome of gilded bronze laurel leaves (FIG. 6.8). Secessionists wanted to abandon historicism and—like Louis Sullivan—strike out in search of new forms of architecture. Emphasizing practicality above all else, they began to erect buildings in concrete and to experiment with glazed tile and ceramics as exterior ornamental elements. These architects also incorporated building hardware prominently into their designs: it was not unusual to reveal the functional bolts and rivets attaching the minimal ornamentation to Secessionist buildings. The Secessionists' motto, emblazoned on their exhibition building: DER ZEIT IHRE KUNST/ DER KUNST IHRE FREIHEIT, To the age its Art; to Art its Freedom.

The Pavilion

The initial impression was of a plain, angular T-shaped structure, built of wood and faced with grayish yellow gypsum shaded with gold, light blue and dark green. "Modern with a classical toning," is the way the Austrian government described the pavilion's architectural style.[11] Guests entered a yellow reception area, which led into fifteen exhibition galleries, all with skylights and decorated in dark green burlap. Twenty-two artists and artisans contributed to the decoration of the building (FIG. 6.9).

FIG. 6.8 *Secession Exhibition Building, Vienna. Photograph by Jack Sidener, ©1993. University of Washington Libraries Digital Collections.*

Inside, Austria had chosen to emphasize and display three aspects of its national culture: railways (to stimulate an interest in tourism); waterways (to demonstrate impressive advances in engineering); and the arts. The third section comprised fine arts, applied arts and handicrafts, representing the work of the Vienna Artists' Association; the recently formed Hagenbund, devoted to Austrian fine arts; and the Polish Artists' Society of Krakow and the Bohemian Artists' Guild. (In 1904, Poland and "Bohemia," then a region of Czechoslovakia, were still part of the Austro-Hungarian empire.)[12]

According to a brochure, Ludwig Bauman was the architect officially cited for the design of the Austrian Pavilion, with his assistant, Joseph Meissner, "substituting him in the superintendence of the works." Spiering's connection and role in this installation is even less visible than with his supervisory

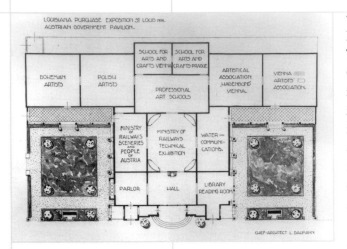

LOUISIANA PURCHASE EXPOSITION ST LOUIS 1904.
AUSTRIAN GOVERNMENT PAVILION.

| BOHEMIAN ARTISTS | POLISH ARTISTS | SCHOOL FOR ARTS AND CRAFTS VIENNA | SCHOOL FOR ARTS AND CRAFTS PRAGUE | ARTISTICAL ASSOCIATION HAGENBUND VIENNA. | VIENNA ARTISTS' ASSOCIATION. |

PROFESSIONAL ART SCHOOLS

MINISTRY OF RAILWAYS SCENERIES AND PEOPLE OF AUSTRIA | MINISTRY OF RAILWAYS TECHNICAL EXHIBITION | WATER COMMUNI-CATIONS.

PARLOR | HALL | LIBRARY READING ROOM

CHEF-ARCHITECT L. BAUMANN

Fɪɢ. 6.9 *Floor plan, Austrian Pavilion. From* **The Austrian Government Pavilion: Louisiana Purchase Exposition, St. Louis, 1904.** *St. Louis Public Library.*

Rɪɢʜᴛ: *Spiering recorded distant and close-up views of the west courtyard of the Austrian Pavilion (top and center); the mural is by Ferdinand Andri of Vienna. The pavilion's east courtyard, photographed looking north, is below.*

work for the French government. But again, he was a likely prospect. Though Ecole-trained, he was a German-American, fluent in his family's second language. Spiering's recent experience in Europe had familiarized him with progressive architectural trends there, and his interest in them may have been enthusiastically conveyed to the Austrians.

Austria did not decide to participate in the LPE until the summer of 1903. Spiering's salaried work on the design staff was concluded that year on December 31, just a week before Austria shipped its pavilion in sections to the United States. By then he was teaching architecture at Washington University and building his own practice. Spiering and crew could not have hoped to be ready by the fair's official opening date of April 30, 1904—nor were many exhibitors—so the formal opening of the building took place on June 2.

That afternoon, following a near contretemps with an angry laborer demanding back pay just minutes before the expected arrival of Miss Alice Roosevelt, daughter of the President of the United States, the building was opened, "with great eclat," reported the *Globe*, "representatives of the best social set in St. Louis having been asked to assist at the initial function."[13]

If Louis Spiering was present that day, the *Globe* did not report it. But we can picture him enjoying an earlier opening reception that spring, held at the French pavilion on April 15 to welcome French Commissioner General Michel Lagrave. It was attended by everyone who had a part in the construction of this New-World Grand Trianon. "The workmen, clad in rough clothes with the baggy trousers characteristic of their class mingled on the easiest terms with their fashionably attired superiors on the staff," a reporter wrote. "In good French wine the delegation pledged allegiance to France and drank to the success of the Exposition."[14]

Chapter   Seven

The Express Office

Spiering and the 'Little Buildings'

During that heady summer of 1901, as the commission of architects first gathered in St. Louis and developed their unique, fan-shaped exposition ground plan, Isaac Taylor came up with a name for the resulting effect: the Main Picture. Within this picture, exhibit palaces would line the axes radiating from the fan point, brought into perfect harmony by Masqueray's decorative elements and landscape architect George Kessler's artful placement of mature trees and massed flower beds. It would be the quintessential City Beautiful.

FIG. 7.1 *Express Office, Louisiana Purchase Exposition. Spiering Album. MHS.*

But the St. Louis World's Fair was, in fact, several pictures telling vastly differing architectural stories. The Plateau of States was a City Vernacular, as each participating state of the union contributed a structure deemed most representative of its history, character or chief industry. The Pike was a City Phantasmagorical. And other sections offered glimpses of a City Moderne.   As architecture critic Robert Duffy has noted: "If you think about the fair, it just screams Beaux-Arts, as far as the central festival building, the colonnades, the restaurant pavilions. But then you find sprinkled around these funny, almost experimental little designs."[1]

Louis Spiering's Express Office was among them (FIG. 7.1). Of his "little buildings" at the World's Fair, the Express Office is the smallest and, in terms of documentation, the most mysterious. We know that this modest structure was originally assigned a pleasant, semi-prominent site, then fell under the long shadow of the prominent Busch brewing family and finally escaped—it appears—to the Model Street near the Lindell Boulevard entrance to the fairgrounds. Spiering's three snapshots of its facades, along with brief descriptive paragraphs found in several exposition guidebooks, are the only clues to the final resting place of the Express Office.

Independent Projects

Though it would be natural to assume that Louis Spiering did all his exposition work under the design staff aegis, it appears that his small buildings and probably his supervisory appointments were independent undertakings. These projects were done for exhibitors that did not sign contracts with the fair until close to the conclusion of—or even after—Spiering's official tour of duty.

How did he earn these commissions? The Express Office may well have come to him as a sidebar to his supervisory

FIG. 7.2 *Express Office, side facade. Spiering Album. MHS.*

position with the French government pavilion project—obtained, we remember, through the American Express Company. Plans for such a building were under discussion by the summer of 1903, as representatives of the nation's major express companies met in St. Louis. The *Globe-Democrat* reported their intention to jointly operate a working exhibit—a model express building (FIG. 7.2 AND 7.3) that would carry on a regular express business "for the accommodation of visitors from all parts of the world"—presumably to allow fairgoers a convenient place to make travel arrangements.[2] Represented were Southern, Wells-Fargo, United States, Adams, National and American express companies.

"The location of express depots on the site for the hauling of express business at the Fair was also discussed," the *Globe* elaborated. "There will be several branch depots distributed over the grounds at points of vantage. The main station will probably be located at the intersection of Skinker Road and the Colorado tracks, where the freight depot will be located. Here an express depot 60 by 500 feet will probably be erected." The model office, however, would fittingly occupy a spot next to the Palace of Transportation on the Plaza of St. Anthony.

So the plans went forward, and we imagine Spiering designing a minute companion piece to Masqueray's gargantuan transportation palace. This building was to be 40 by 80 feet, according to the *Globe*, "of pleasing architecture in keeping with the buildings of the main picture, in which it will have a place, and will be elegant and elaborate in its interior appointments."[3] The estimated cost was $15,000–$20,000. The site information was transmitted to mapmaker Woodward and Tiernan, then engaged in the creation of ground plan reproductions that could be used in guidebooks and as advertising pieces. These maps were only minimally updated after 1903. Consequently, most versions show the Express Office at its original appointed site on the Plaza of St. Anthony.

FIG. 7.3 *Express Office, front facade. Spiering Album. MHS.*

Around the Mulberry Busch

But by February 1904, a competitor for the St. Anthony site had made his voice heard. "Mr. Gussie Busch,"[4] according to the February 4 minutes of the exposition Grounds and Buildings Committee, wished to erect a restaurant there. The committee was not inclined to approve. But Busch pursued the matter, and the committee capitulated, provided the restaurant would not extend farther south than 125 feet of its northern perimeter. Busch demanded additional space on the plaza. On March 12, the committee voted no, and requested that Busch notify Isaac Taylor within the week if he "desires the location assigned."[5]

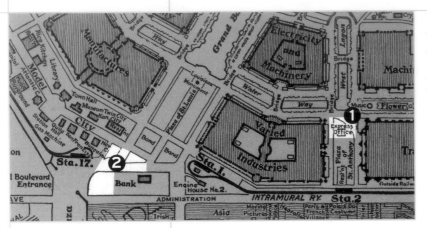

FIG. 7.4 *Map detail, eastern section of fairgrounds. The original location of the Express Office is shown at #1; its eventual site in the vicinity of #2. Private collection.*

Reading between the lines, we gather that Busch yet again pressed his case, for the committee, on April 12, resorted to a Solomon-like solution: "The Insurance Companies have ruled that there be no building between the aforesaid Exhibit Palaces [Transportation and Varied Industries]. It was therefore resolved that the Express Office now being erected in said space be removed and that no other building of any character whatever be permitted on the Plaza of St. Anthony."[6]

With the fair's opening less than three weeks away, Spiering must have been forced to drastically revise his plan, or perhaps start from scratch. The Model City—itself pruned severely by the costs of its ambitious original scope—became the site of the Express Office (FIG. 7.4).

Was it the same 40-by-80-foot office planned for the Plaza of St. Anthony? Spiering's three snapshots are enigmatic. "It's like French railroad station architecture you see about this period of time," said architectural historian Osmund Overby in 2003. "Generic, simple, functional, more or less modern, with a little bit of decoration. Very practical, too, with good, deep eaves so [patrons] can stand outside waiting for [the] train, or for the baggage office to open."

"What sets it apart," said Overby, "is the quality of the proportions and relationship of the decoration to the massing of the whole. This sort of thing came almost instinctively to architects well trained in design."[7]

Louis/Louis

Louis LaBeaume's Travelers Protective Association building is another small structure that underwent major surgery between its first emergence from the drawing board and its final incarnation on the fairgrounds. By mid-September 1902, the TPA was growing impatient for a site allocation in its assigned area, the Plateau of States. In the politest terms, representative C. H. Wickard reminded the exposition officials that the TPA had been the first organization to raise and tender their subscription to the World's Fair fund.[8] And indeed, as we have seen, they were the first to publish a building design, created for them by Louis LaBeaume in the summer of 1901.

LaBeaume's original plan was for a two-story structure, 176 feet wide, with an imposing colonnaded entry that welcomed visitors into a spacious clublike retreat (FIG. 7.5). It was to contain a smoking room, lounge, ladies' parlor, assembly hall with stage, dining room and billiard room.[9] The estimated cost was $100,000. As for its design, observed architecture critic Robert Duffy, assessing it a century later: "It's almost slavishly symmetrical, its whole organization is very related to the Beaux-Arts. It could be translated into a Portland Place [exclusive St. Louis gated street] residence."[10]

On October 2, 1902, the TPA received its World's Fair site allocation. LaBeaume's building would stand at the northern end of the Plateau States, facing north on

a slight northward slope, its rear to the massive flight cage installed by the Smithsonian Institution, a still-popular aviary known today as the 1904 Flight Cage of the St. Louis Zoo. Was the site problematic? Was LaBeaume's original design overblown and over budget? Or was it never seriously intended as the final product? We don't know. But by May 9, 1903, a new TPA design appeared in the *St. Louis Globe-Democrat*, half the size of the original, estimated to cost $15,000, "a very modern adaptation of the French renaissance."[11] The illustration clearly bears Louis LaBeaume's signature. What it also bears, in part, is a passing resemblance to the West Restaurant Pavilion (FIG. 7.6).

FIG. 7.5 *Traveler's Protective Association building, Louisiana Purchase Exposition. Above, Louis LaBeaume's original design. From* World's Fair Bulletin. *St. Louis Public Library.*

The lower elevation of this TPA structure is distinctly Secessionist in feeling, a relatively blank facade contrasted with a decorative dentil cornice and frieze of rosettes. Then, however, a confectionery roofline sends the design in a different direction, one reminiscent of Masqueray's (or Spiering's?) work on Art Hill. As noted by Esley Hamilton: "The Travelers Protective Association and the West Restaurant building...are both designed as three-dimensional sculptural objects; the

FIG. 7.6 *Traveler's Protective Association building, LaBeaume's final version. Photograph. St. Louis Public Library.*

roof is actually part of the design because of the way the roof rises up in the central tower."[12] Hamilton speculates that the sloping site, allowing the roof to be seen from above, may have inclined the designer to an ornamental treatment.

Remembering LaBeaume's less than complimentary reminiscence of Masqueray, we wonder if Masqueray proffered unwelcome guidance to the second design of the TPA structure. LaBeaume does not mention either version of the TPA building in his World's Fair memoir, expunging it from his record much as he did Louis Spiering.[13]

The best remembrance of the TPA building, then, may be as the scene of an enthusiastic Travelers Protective Association

Day fete in June 1904, when three thousand members
convened at the site. The party was pronounced a huge success,
though a dry one, because once again there was a problem
with the help: "The smiles will fade from the faces of the
temperance society members throughout the country when
they read that an unusual spirituous drought was due to the
failure of the caterer to make his appearance until the reception
was practically over," noted a reporter. "He was due at the
building at 3 o'clock, but did not show up until after 4. He was
sent away by the reception committee."[14]

No corresponding account tells of a reception to mark
the dedication of Louis Spiering's model Express Office. But
it is probably safe to assume that if the express companies did
celebrate, they did not serve local brew at their party.

The Palais on the Pike

I t was the place to hear ragtime, which was banned from the main fairgrounds. It was hootchy-kootchy heaven. It was the Pike, a mile-long amusement arcade crammed with nearly three dozen attractions, eager fairgoers and rowdy, raw-throated barkers.

We have to ask: what was a nice designer like Louis Spiering doing in a place like this? For there, smack in the middle (FIG. 8.1), close to the spot where Hunting in the Ozarks stood cheek by jowl with Hagenbeck's Zoological Paradise and Animal Circus, across the street from Mysterious Asia and three doors to the west, between the Paris & the French Village and the Infant Incubator, stood the Palais du Costume...Louis Spiering's architectural contribution to the Pike.

We really don't know how he landed there. We do know that this building is the only Spiering exposition design for which an architectural rendering, albeit a copy, survives. And it shows us that even when an architect like Louis goes honky-tonk, he goes first-class.

The Premise

According to promoters, the Palais du Costume was a $625,000 display of gowns and other attire that traced the history of apparel from ancient Rome to the new twentieth century. The concession was touted as educational: each costume was modeled on a mannequin representing a famous historical figure of her era; the mannequins, in turn, were posed in lifelike settings "with all the environments, such as furniture, interior

OPPOSITE: *Spiering's photograph of the Arts and Crafts-influenced open-air cafe, Palais du Costume. Spiering Album. MHS.*

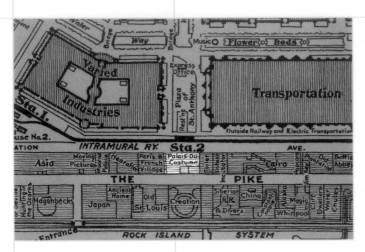

FIG. 8.1 *Map detail, northern boundary of fairgrounds: the Palais du Costume on the Pike. Private collection.*

FIG. 8.2 *"The Eve of the Coronation" featured an appreciative Napoleon admiring his wife, Josephine, in her coronation robes. From* The Greatest of Expositions. *Private collection.*

decorations, tapestries and ornaments reproduced in every detail with the utmost care and exactitude."[1]

Visitors could see Josephine on the eve of Napoleon's coronation, modeling for her husband the sumptuous, ermine-trimmed robe in which she would be crowned Empress of France (FIG. 8.2). "The purple field is sown with golden bees," reported a member of the World's Fair press corps, "and encircling the train is a wreath of imperial emblems worked in pearls."[2] Noting that the "average woman would be taxed to support" the weight of this gown, the writer added that this replica, duplicated in the materials of the original, had cost $40,000. In addition, the chamber in which Napoleon, Josephine and their courtiers appeared was furnished in costly Napoleonic-era antiques.[3]

"The Eve of the Coronation" was one of thirty tableaux. Others were "The Field of the Cloth of Gold" (Henry VIII and Francis I); "Byzantium—Homage to the Empress"; and "A Roman Interior." Promoters claimed that the Palais had been a sensation in Paris and London, and to boost its appeal to Americans, the Palais du Costume Co., in partnership with Barr's dry goods store of St. Louis, arranged for an array of contemporary fashions to be modeled daily by eight young women representing a number of states of the union. Barr's collaborated with New York importers of Paris gowns to bring in street dresses, reception and wedding gowns, as well as the latest in hats, gloves and parasols.

From Paris to St. Louis

The 1904 Palais was successor to an attraction at the Paris
Exposition of 1900; the reported "sensation" had bankrupted
its prominent dressmaker creator, M. Felix, and was sold to
Earls Court, the famous London exhibition center. On May 12,
1903, the Louisiana Purchase Exposition Company Executive
Committee approved a contract with the Palais du Costume
Company, formed by nine local investors to bring the Palais to
the Pike. Soon thereafter, the company posted a $20,000 bond
covering agreements in the concession contract with the LPE.[4]

It was around this time that Louis Spiering, along with
St. Louis architects Ernest Helfensteller and William Hirsch,
received a commission to design the Palais du Costume (FIG.
8.3). "Mr. Spiering," reported the *World's Fair Bulletin* in
November 1903, after the building plans had been let for bid,
"says that the Palais du Costume will be an original modern
exposition building, and at the same time have the charm of
the Italian renaissance with the strength of detail of the French
renaissance."[5] The building's cost was estimated at $30,000.
Designing for the Pike presented Spiering with unprecedented
challenges. Visitors would view and perceive Pike concessions
differently than they did the splendors of the main fairgrounds.
On the Pike, the eye would be forced to abandon its leisurely
travel across long, scenic approaches, and adjust to what was
essentially a tunnel. Consequently, a visitor could take in a
total facade in only a limited fashion, backing off at an angle
to view it in three-quarter profile.

Another architect might have bowed to these limitations,
and/or privately conceded that few visited the Pike to critique
its architecture. Spiering appeared unconcerned. Perhaps he
had seen the original 1900 Palais in Paris and considered it a
serious exhibit, for he designed a dignified, Secessionist-tinged
structure that has, as Osmund Overby observed, "a real sense
of a built building."[6] It could have held its own in any setting.

The Palais du Costume was a building of 175 by 150 feet.
Though it appeared as a triptych—an impression reinforced
by the massing of its triple-arched entry in the central bay—a
perfectly harmonizing annex completed the western end,
housing the Café Palais du Costume. Strong horizontal lines in
roof and decoration tied the elements together, and emphasized

PALAIS · DV · COSTVME
LOVISIANA · PVRCHASE · EXPOSITION

FIG. 8.3 *"An original modern exposition building" as envisioned by its creator. Drawing by Louis Spiering.*

FIGS. 8.4 AND 8.5 *Art nouveau on the Pike: "Hereafter and Creation" concessions by Carson, Hudson and Weatherwax. From* The Universal Exposition of 1904, *private collection; and St Louis Public Library.* MHS.

the building's Secessionist influence. Spiering's interest in Secessionism may be further observed in the unusual flat, deep-eaved decorative roof atop the central bay of the main structure. This roof design is echoed in the deeply projecting trusses atop the Café section, though this portion, with its open gallery below the trusses, is more than a little reminiscent of Arts and Crafts architecture of the period, such as Greene and Greene's 1907 Gamble House in Pasadena, California.

If Spiering was aiming for a subtle nod to Secessionism, another partnership of Pike architects, Carson, Hudson and Weatherwax, adopted the trend wholesale. Two doors east of the Palais stood their "Hereafter," a concession based on Dante's *Inferno* (FIG. 8.4). Inside, visitors passed through the seven circles of hell, depicted in "grewsome" accuracy, and finally emerging "through the Grove of Daphne to Paradise."[7] The facade of "Hereafter" owes much to the new design work emanating from Austria.

Carson, Hudson and Weatherwax designed twenty Pike concessions.[8] For "Creation," a cheerier concept directly across from the Palais, they turned to Secessionism's cousin, art nouveau (FIG. 8.5). Fronting a bright blue dome, the facade of "Creation" evokes French architect Jules Lavirotte's famously flamboyant residential design at 29 Avenue Rapp

FIGS. 8.4

FIGS. 8.5

FIG. 8.6 *Art nouveau in Paris: 29 Avenue Rapp, a residence designed by Jules Lavirotte, ca. 1901. Photograph by Ellen Schmidt, 2002. Private collection.*

in Paris (FIG. 8.6). "Creation" was likely the only example of French art nouveau architecture on the fairgrounds.

Faded Glory

By October 1904, the Palais du Costume was in financial trouble, just as its Parisian predecessor. The company reported that it had been "operating at a great loss," and proposed to pay all bills rendered by the LPE Company, except for $3,750 in ground rent. The company's proposal was accepted by the executive committee.[9]

As closing day, December 1, drew near, public attention turned toward long-term restoration of the fairgrounds, starting with the disposal of exposition buildings and treasures within. Any building made of staff, of course, would be demolished. But other structures, such as the state buildings, could be had for extremely attractive prices, dismantled and reassembled elsewhere. The public was slow to respond, prompting snickers from the press.

On November 24, a new after-the-fair story broke: "Permanent Pike an Assured Fact." By December 9, however, the idea was abandoned, and the concessions went on the block, just as their upper-crust neighbors to the south. Contents of the buildings were sold, portions of interiors salvaged and demolition bids were sought.[10] On December 20, the *St. Louis Globe-Democrat* reported progress on the clearing of the Pike. Concessions were in various stages of dismantlement or demolition. Only the Palais du Costume lagged significantly: "Exhibits still in the building; structure has not been sold; no satisfactory bids received."

For a long list of entrepreneurs, the LPE was not the bonanza they'd hoped. But for Louis Spiering, the Palais du Costume was obviously a success: he made more photographs of it (FIG. 8.7 AND 8.8) than of any other structure at the fair.

FIGS. 8.7 AND 8.8 *Two of Spiering's twelve views of the Palais du Costume: "a real sense of a built building." Both from Spiering Album. MHS.*

Chapter Nine

Up in Lights

The American De Forest Wireless Telegraph Tower

"The staccato crackle of our spark, when purposely unmuffled, brought them swarming from all over that end of the Exposition grounds."

LEE DE FOREST, *"Father of Radio"*

ireless telegraphy—the forerunner of radio—sent Morse code signals through the air. In 1904 it was the hottest thing in technology, the focus of growing attention that had ignited when Guglielmo Marconi, experimenting in Italy, made the first successful transmission of radio waves in 1895. In 1899, on board a ship off New York Harbor, he used wireless to report on the America's Cup yacht races for the *New York Herald*. And in 1901, he transmitted a signal across the Atlantic. The public was fascinated.

But by then, Marconi had several competitors, among them Reginald T. Fessenden, John S. Stone and Lee De Forest. None worked more doggedly or craved recognition more fiercely than De Forest. And though it was Marconi who was wined and dined by St. Louis fair officials in hopes that he would be the one to operate the first wireless exhibit at a World's Fair, it was the De Forest name that eventually blazed above the fairgrounds, outlined in electric lights against the steel tower that sent voodoo signals into the ether. Louis Spiering would take on the responsibility of bringing De Forest's tower—a prominent futuristic symbol—into visual harmony with an otherwise historicist fairground (FIG. 9.1 and 9.2).

FIG. 9.1 *American De Forest Wireless Telegraph Tower. From* **The Greatest of Expositions.** *Private collection.*

A Craving for Fame

Lee De Forest (1873–1961) traced his fascination with wireless telegraphy to his adolescence in Talladega, Alabama. There, his father, a stern and remote Congregational clergyman, had moved the family when he became president of Talladega College, a school chartered in 1869 for children of freed slaves. The De Forest family was shunned by disapproving white citizens of the town, so for companionship young Lee relied on his brother and sister, and on his scientific experiments. He also began a journal, which he kept for decades. The entries shift from smarmy moralizing to self-aggrandizement to bald-faced revelations of avarice—all recorded in prose of deepest purple, the tone of De Forest's prolific writings from the earliest days into his final years.

De Forest was expected to enter the clergy, but rejected religious study in favor of science, determined to win fame as an inventor. He attended prep school in Massachusetts, and then entered Yale where, biographers unfailingly point out, he was voted "nerviest" and "homeliest" in his class. De Forest also received one vote for "smartest" and sixteen for "thinks he is."[1] In 1899, De Forest earned a Ph.D. from Yale's Sheffield School of Science, writing his doctoral dissertation on Hertzian waves. Then De Forest took a series of industry-related jobs. Working for others by day, he logged endless hours of free time in wireless experimentation and development of two moderately successful devices. In 1901, De Forest and two associates obtained backing to compete with Marconi as the Italian inventor again covered the America's Cup races. The rival wireless systems jammed one another, according to historian Susan Douglas, and the yacht race results "had to be reported by flags and crude hand signals."[2] But no matter to De Forest: he had enjoyed a taste of public acclaim, and, in his own mind, at least, seriously undercut his archrival, Marconi.

In 1902, De Forest—hungry, shabbily dressed and nearly penniless—met Texan Abraham White, a flamboyant and smooth-talking stock promoter. *Né* Schwartz, the German word for "black," White was almost a caricature of a snake oil salesman. "White's hair and mustache were flaming red; his eyes of china blue," journalist Samuel Lubell reported years later in *The Saturday Evening Post*. "He wore patent-leather shoes, a silk hat, a flower in his buttonhole, a handsome gold

watch chain, a pear-shaped pearl scarf pin and a diamond ring that was not too big. He smoked corkscrew-shaped cigars which he handed out freely, was never without a fat roll of $100 gold certificates, which he peeled off with the easy indifference of an actor handling stage money."[3]

Grasping immediately the profitable implications of an alliance with De Forest, White invited him to an elegant restaurant luncheon meeting. In a tour de force worthy of Professor Harold Hill or Max Bialystock, White dazzled the young scientist with delicacies served from chafing dishes and, of course, the roll of gold certificates. Handing him a $100 bill with a flourish, White sealed their "partnership" in the new De Forest Wireless Telegraph Company. White would assume the presidency, and De Forest would take the title of vice president and scientific director.

FIG. 9.2 *The tower formed an expedient but aesthetically controversial closure to the axis extending northeast from the East Restaurant Pavilion. Photograph. St. Louis Public Library.*

"Suckers"

The appearance of this bountiful backer thrilled and relieved De Forest. Now the business end of the enterprise was in capable hands, and De Forest's own financial woes were over, leaving him free to concentrate on his wireless network. Working feverishly, he set up stations in New York City, Coney Island, Buffalo, Cleveland and Chicago.

White, of course, had no intention of expanding a functional wireless network. He wanted to make fast money and had the cunning to do it. First, he established a corporate office on Wall Street as a front for the organization that consisted only of himself, De Forest, a few technicians and some stock salesmen. To attract attention, he outfitted an automobile with a small wireless station, which he parked on the streets below, where De Forest could be seen transmitting stock market quotations to a nearby Dow Jones office.

In addition to orchestrating promotional stunts, White shrewdly manipulated the press. He churned out news releases with bogus claims about the De Forest company;

FIG. 9.3 *Hard at work on the fairgrounds: Lee De Forest (left) transmits a wireless signal, as Abraham White assumes a characteristic stance, making money off a colleague's back. MHS.*

unquestioning editors ran the releases word for word, generating headlines that White could quote in his lavish sales brochures.

The brochures were then used on site whenever White established a new tower "station." Moving about the eastern half of the United States, White typically spent a few thousand dollars on the construction of a new tower, where he staged showy demonstrations, sold many times his start-up costs in worthless stock, and moved on, abandoning the tower and its investors. His modus operandi was successful. Although the business world proved wary of investing in wireless, the tech-happy public, eager for another Bell Telephone-caliber opportunity, was another story. Everyone wanted to get in on the ground floor.

And what of De Forest's role in all this? Historians are rarely sympathetic to him; the assessment of his degree of culpability ranges from marginally aware to full-blown accomplice. An early February 1902 entry in De Forest's journal does not speak favorably: "Soon, we believe, the suckers will begin to bite! Fine fishing weather, now that the oil fields have played out. 'Wireless' is the bait to use at present. May we stock our string before the wind veers, & the sucker shoals are swept out to sea!"[4]

De Forest would later learn that he, too, had been a sucker (FIG. 9.3). But in 1902, he willingly accepted his modest salary of $20 per week.[5] It proved sufficient to keep him comfortable, and his name on the company letterhead as a cover for White.

In fact, when De Forest learned that Abraham White, a man he regarded as a "brother," intended to install a wireless telegraph tower at the Louisiana Purchase Exposition of 1904, the jubilant De Forest felt that he had come full circle. Once upon a time, he had said a forlorn goodbye to the Chicago exposition. "Little then did I imagine," De Forest recorded, "that eleven years later, at the next great World's Fair Exposition, [my] name in incandescence would emblazon the loftiest tower."[6]

Edging out Marconi

Marconi, however, was still the pre-eminent name in wireless. In September 1903, the Italian inventor and several associates visited the directors of the St. Louis World's

Fair, who were keen to add the Marconi name to their list of attractions. The Marconi entourage was taken to the fairgrounds in a private trolley car and then to a round of festivities at several clubs. By the conclusion of the whirlwind visit, Marconi had been assigned a twenty-five thousand square-foot location just east of Art Hill, on which he would establish a wireless station. "Aerial communications will be flashed from exposition to distant corners of the old world," declared a newspaper headline. "Inventor much pleased."[7]

But the inventor evidently was less pleased to learn that the LPE was also in negotiations with the De Forest company. According to Susan Douglas: "Although the Marconi Company initially had exclusive rights to display wireless at the St. Louis Exposition, [Abraham] White succeeded in convincing the fair authorities that an American wireless company should also be represented."[8] White had had good luck playing the nationalism card in the past. It worked again on the LPE Executive Committee with unexpectedly advantageous results. Marconi, who did not want to be seen as a competitor of De Forest, and especially not as a colleague, withdrew. Now the newly renamed *American* De Forest Wireless Telegraph Company would dominate the fair's wireless operations and exhibits, and by February 4, 1904, had submitted a drawing of the proposed tower for approval by the LPE Executive Committee.

Enter Louis Spiering

As Louis Spiering rang out the old year on December 31, 1903, he concluded his salaried employment on the World's Fair design staff, though he was still deeply involved with projects on the fairgrounds. In just a few weeks, sections of the Austrian Pavilion would begin arriving by train, and work on the French Pavilion was only about seventy percent completed. The Palais du Costume was at roughly the same point, and the Express Office was on schedule—or so Spiering thought—for spring completion on the Plaza of St. Anthony.[9] Spiering, then, was working with four exposition clients, plus whatever private clients had begun patronizing his architectural practice at the Chemical Building in downtown St. Louis. He had become active in the St. Louis chapter of the American Institute of Architects. And as soon as the Christmas

vacation ended, he would begin
his second semester as instructor
of architecture at Washington
University, presiding over an *atelier*-
modeled evening course that met
twice weekly.

Spiering was about to add one
more obligation to the list, courtesy
of White and De Forest. In taking
on their wireless telegraph tower,
Spiering found himself responsible
for not only the most traditional
(French Pavilion) and the most
avant garde (Austrian Pavilion)
structures, but also for the tallest: at
three hundred feet, the tower would
dwarf even Festival Hall.

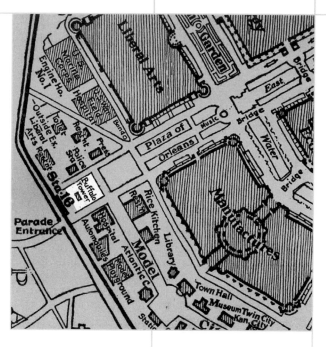

The steel structure itself
was inherited—Abraham White had spent $10,000 on an
observation tower that formerly overlooked Niagara Falls, to
be reconstructed near the parade entrance to the fairgrounds
(FIG. 9.4). Isaac Taylor had chosen this site, saying it would
provide "artistic closure" for the long axis stretching
northeast from the East Restaurant Pavilion.[10] Spiering's job
was to unite the elements of the structure—base, steel tower
and crown—and bring the total effect into harmony with other
fair architecture.

FIG. 9.4 *Map detail.
White's installation
appeared on LPE maps
as the "Buffalo Tower."
Private collection.*

At the same time, Spiering needed to express the
trailblazing essence of the tower. Thus he seized a unique
opportunity. While most fair architects had reiterated classicist
themes of fairs gone by, and a few had adopted contemporary
trends, Louis Spiering would present his vision of tomorrow.

"Our New Century"

Spiering's World's Fair album contains two photographs
of the wireless tower base, framed with powerful immediacy,
showing this project as an ultimate concours (FIG. 9.5 and 9.6).
In the first shot, he gives us a dead-on view of the tower at
ground level: a square building whose sides are relieved only
by a hooded triple arch. This structure is so preternaturally
spare that Spiering's Palais du Costume, in contrast, seems

FIG. 9.5 AND 9.6
Spiering's snapshots record his most futuristic designs on the fairgrounds. Spiering Album. MHS.

ornate. Yet the ivory staff facade, very likely constructed around the weight-bearing steel base of the actual tower, offers a nod to the "Great White City" tradition of the LPE. The triple arch echoes Spiering's Palais, which in turn paid probable homage to Masqueray's Palace of Transportation.

The second image is arguably the cleverest commentary in Spiering's album. Shifting the tower base to the left side of the frame, he places its now undeniably futuristic profile prominently in the foreground, composing a shot that leads our eye along a curved path to a distant terminus: the barely discernible East Restaurant Pavilion. Spiering is having fun here, enjoying a little photographic triumph as he shows the mind-boggling contrast of architectural styles in which he worked at the St. Louis World's Fair. "Look," he seems to say. "Way up there is the old order, the status quo. And here, staring us in the face, is our new century."

But why only two images in Spiering's album? And why are they both of the base? The supreme height of the tower was one of its great claims to fame. Any fairgoer with a simple camera could photograph the wireless telegraph tower from top to near-bottom, albeit at a distance. If Spiering had charge of the total structure, didn't he want to preserve a record?

Not if he had been disappointed in the tower's final execution. We begin to suspect that is exactly what happened when we view others' photographs of the tower as a whole. For they show that the tower's dome is out of balance—incongruously homespun, almost a grandstand. It could have been snatched at the last minute from a nearby state fair, and plopped down on the De Forest tower's upper deck while Spiering was occupied elsewhere. It does not look like Spiering's work.

There is compelling evidence, however, that Spiering originally designed a dome every bit as forward-looking as his tower base—evidence in the form of an architectural rendering that appears on the cover of a promotional brochure from the LPE (FIG. 9.7). This is a drawing of the full tower ensemble, and it tells a dramatically different story. Here the dome is an arresting, almost Buck Rogeresque statement of unity with the tower base.

Is this Spiering's drawing? Probably. The accuracy of the surrounding fairgrounds suggests that the artist was intimately familiar with the LPE ground plan. And the perspective is much like the one later chosen by Spiering in his tower photograph that contrasts old architecture with new.

While it's great fun to speculate about this fantasy dome and the reasons it never materialized (time? money?), there is a more pressing motive for hoping that the brochure drawing was made by Louis Spiering. If it is his work, it becomes a link to an important piece of Spieringiana that was lost decades ago, a pencil and pastel drawing titled "An Architectural Apotheosis of St. Louis." Spiering displayed his "Apotheosis" in 1910 in a St. Louis Artists' Guild architectural exhibit. A reviewer described the work: "[It] suggests the historical development of the city, from the Indian tent near the lonely river, to the magnificence of the World's Fair architecture, and daringly predicted structures yet to come."[11]

How useful it would be to see Louis Spiering's vision of "structures yet to come." The loss of this monumental work is a continuing disappointment to architectural historians, for Spiering's "Apotheosis" could well indicate the directions in which his design career might have proceeded had he enjoyed a longer life. But if we can look to the drawing on the De Forest brochure as an indicator, we reconnect with Spiering's boldest imaginings.

FIG. 9.7 *Illustration, probably by Spiering, shows the original design of the De Forest Wireless Telegraph Tower dome. From brochure,* The De Forest Wireless Telegraph System. *St. Louis Public Library.*

Winning Top Honors

The De Forest Wireless Telegraph Tower was a popular destination. Fairgoers rode its two electric elevators to the uppermost observation deck, where they thrilled to the matchless view of fairgrounds fanning out three hundred feet below. Intrigued, perplexed, unbelieving, they watched De Forest at the transmitter as he sent World's Fair news to the downtown editorial offices of the *St. Louis Star* and the *St. Louis Post-Dispatch*. The tower was only a part of the De Forest company's wireless exhibits. In the nearby Palace of Electricity, the company displayed its wireless-equipped automobiles. And a second, far less imposing tower, outfitted for long distance transmissions, was situated to the southwest, between Jerusalem and the Boer War exhibit.

From there, the De Forest company made its biggest splash: on September 6, it successfully sent a message 105 miles overland to Springfield, Illinois; ten days later, De Forest surpassed himself by transmitting a congratulatory message three hundred miles from the Railway Exchange Building in Chicago to a waiting Abraham White in St. Louis. Trumpeted the *Post-Dispatch*: WIRELESS TELEGRAPHY ANNIHILATES SPACE BETWEEN ST. LOUIS AND CHICAGO.[12]

De Forest had timed this feat to coincide with Electricity Day at the fair. On hand to witness his triumph were heretofore skeptical delegates of the Electrical Congress, as well as the jury of awards. The De Forest exhibit won the grand prize for superiority in the transmission of wireless messages, and the gold medal for excellence of its installation and the perfection of its instruments.[13]

White, characteristically, stood ready with promises for reporters: "President White...said that this remarkable feat proved beyond question the feasibility of extending the De Forest system to all parts of the world," citing immediate plans to link the company's new stations in Omaha and Fort Worth with "all intermediate points of importance," and to establish links of communication along the Pacific Coast.[14]

The End of a Beautiful Friendship

The company's fulfillment of its contractual obligations to the LPE Company, however, fell short of its technological performance. By the close of the fair, American De Forest, with a debt of $5,817.97, had joined a list of deadbeat concessionaires owing the LPE a total of $292,000. The executive committee voted on January 9, 1905 to sue American De Forest and to temporarily maintain the tower.[15] The abandoned structure already was proving a hazard; just before Christmas, a fourteen-year-old boy, acting on a wager, had fallen from the tower's topmost flagpole and escaped death only by his serendipitous plunge through a scuttle hole in the roof below.[16]

Washington University reportedly considered purchasing the tower to use as an observatory, but the plan was dropped.[17] Eventually, the tower—sans its Spiering-designed Tomorrowland base— was moved to Creve Coeur Park in the far reaches of west St. Louis County, where it served as observation deck for the surrounding lake and parkland.[18]

By 1906, the LPE Executive Committee voted to write the De Forest Company's debt off the books. The same year, White did much the same to De Forest. The scientist had fled to Canada with the expectation that White would pay a heavy fine levied against him in a patent infringement suit. Instead, according to historian Tom Lewis, White froze De Forest out of American De Forest, transferring all assets including patents—but none of the liabilities—to a newly formed company. De Forest was left with only $1,000 in severance pay, all of the old company's debts and a single invention deemed worthless by White et al.[19]

As it happened, the invention was the audion: "a new method of detecting wireless waves with a small incandescent electric lamp or tube"[20]—in actuality a primitive vacuum tube, the device that brought radio into being. The audion was based on research by Thomas Edison, yet De Forest claimed it as his own, along with the nickname "Father of Radio," which he made the title of his self-serving autobiography.

As for Abraham White, in decades to follow, he as well as Lee De Forest would lead lives of seeming karmic acceleration, gaining and losing fortunes in rapid cycles of shady dealings and retribution.

And whether Louis Spiering fell afoul of the erstwhile partners in the collection of his architect's fee...we shall never know.

1904 and Beyond

At Louis Spiering's memorial service, a friend observed: "to an unusual degree, in him was combined the culture of the old world with the enthusiasm and vitality of the new."[1] Spiering used these qualities to full advantage in his work at the St. Louis World's Fair of 1904. He was ideally suited to it, because the exposition, too, was a microcosm of Old- and New-World sensibilities.

Spiering brought to the great exposition his Beaux-Arts experience coupled with the still broader perspective of his cosmopolitan family. He could easily connect with the sensibilities of foreign architectural dignitaries, and his fluency in French and German promoted better understanding among these finely tuned and harried professionals as they struggled to meet their deadlines. Perhaps foremost, Spiering could comprehend the frustrations of Emmanuel Masqueray, his superior, and probably provided a sounding board for that most beleaguered architect on the fairgrounds—even as he intuited the master's visions of canals, bridges and lamps illuminating the walkways.

The fair, in turn, was good to its First Design Assistant. It appears that Spiering arrived in St. Louis with his course plotted. Clearly he envisioned a future as an American *patron*—building a thriving practice while raising the standards of his profession through teaching. The St. Louis World's Fair gave him a solid base from which to launch his ambitions. Spiering's close association with Masqueray, who had risen along that same trajectory a decade earlier, allowed him to observe and consult the master.

OPPOSITE: *Detail, residence at 36 Westmoreland Place. Photograph by Howard Porter, 2003.*

And the fair was a superb vantage point from which Spiering could observe the ins and outs of the city that had grown up in his fourteen-year absence. How did things work here? Who were the principal players? Who were his future clientele? A young architect paying close attention could learn much from watching behind the scenes.

Honored at the Fair

At the same time, Spiering gained an opportunity to size up his competition. His design staff position brought him into familiarity with the principal architects of the city. Probably most significant to Spiering, the fair allowed him to make his national debut as their peer: a jury selected his work for display in the architecture exhibit in the Palace of Fine Arts.

As one of just seventy-three American architect exhibitors, Spiering saw his work positioned among that of the most prominent architects of the day, such as Cope and Stewardson, Greene and

FIG. 10.1 *Spiering-designed residence at 6253 Washington Avenue. MHS.*

Greene, and Cass Gilbert.[2] Though Spiering submitted five entries, all from the Ecole, the jury passed on his contemporary designs, including his diploma project, "A Mansion for a Rich Amateur of Music," which had been exhibited in the Paris Salon of 1903. Inexplicably, jurors chose instead an example of a different kind of work from the Ecole: Spiering's measured drawings of plan and section of St. Julien-le-Pauvre, a medieval church that is one of the oldest in Paris' Latin Quarter.

This choice may have been a disappointment to Spiering, but he could take satisfaction in the exposition's final benefit to him, something of no little import to a young architect and of great interest to later architectural historians. The fair allowed Spiering to produce his earliest examples of work in St. Louis, and the only examples of experimental work his brief remaining future would permit. His freelance "little buildings"—the Palais du Costume, Express Office and especially the American De Forest Wireless Telegraph Tower—clearly indicate that the young architect's interest had been piqued by stirrings abroad.

By the turn of the twentieth century, a new, sleeker, rectilinear architectural style, predictor of the coming modernist movement, was proliferating in parts of Britain and Europe. In the United States, the unadorned, little-appreciated Austrian Pavilion at the St. Louis World's Fair of 1904 was an early symbol for those who could and would see: historicism had developed a hairline crack at the foundation. Louis Spiering's World's Fair album, with its multiple images of the Secessionist Austrian installation, proves that he saw quite clearly.

Indeed, by 1934, the year of Cass Gilbert's death, eclecticism was all but over—considered not only stylistically but morally wrong, as Osmund Overby has commented. From Louis Sullivan and Frank Lloyd Wright, he said, we got the lesson that eclectic architecture represented a "kind of failure on our part, that we weren't true to ourselves but instead put up these great shams and lived a kind of vicarious and fictitious life within them."[3]

Fig. 10.2 *Spiering-designed residence at 39 Kingsbury Place. MHS.*

So Louis Spiering returned to St. Louis at an interesting moment. After the fair, he had less than a decade to architecturally declare himself. His post-fair work deserves thorough analysis; still, a brief tour of the highlights gives some indication of Spiering's sympathies.

Another Direction — Spiering's Residences

In Spiering's remaining years, he produced neither the Beaux-Arts palazzi still favored in St. Louis' gated residential private places, nor additional Secession-influenced structures.[4]

Instead, Spiering designed in a variety of styles for a cross-section of residential clients throughout Compton Heights, the Central West End, University City and Webster Groves. Many of these projects were completed during his brief partnership with George W. Hellmuth (1870–1955).[5]

Spiering's residential clients were primarily upper middle-class industrialists, company presidents and business men, with a few professionals in the mix—a physician, a dentist and one Republican Congressman, Henry Stewart Caulfield, who later served as governor of Missouri from 1929 to 1933, and as judge in the St. Louis Court of Appeals. Caulfield's 1909 two-story brick house at 6253 Washington Avenue in Parkview Place, is among the more formally symmetrical Spiering designs (FIG. 10.1). So are his residences on Kingsbury Place: #39, for clothing manufacturer Nathan Friedman (1909), described as Georgian-Federal Revival by writer Julius K. Hunter (FIG. 10.2); and at the Mediterranean villa-style #42, designed in 1907 for lace importer Sigmund Glaser.[6]

Arts and Crafts

Spiering, however, appeared to prefer the Arts and Crafts style, a movement originating in England and loosely associated with art nouveau/Secessionism, that celebrated the integrity of handicraft and the use of honest,

FIG. 10.3 *Spiering-designed residence at 2908 Accomac. MHS.*

natural materials. Examples may be seen at 2908 Accomac Avenue in Compton Heights, designed in 1907 for Lincoln K. Loy, president of Loy-Lange Box and Lumber Company; and nearby, west of Grand Boulevard, at 4242 Flora Place, a comparatively diminutive cottage of enormous charm crafted for Thomas W. Davis, president of the O'Connor Market Reporter Company (FIG. 10.3 AND FIG. 10.4). In what Esley Hamilton calls a "Spiering mini-district" on Princeton Place in University City, a trio of residences at #7, #8 and #18 show the architect's versatility within the Arts and Crafts genre. "The Budke house [#7] combines Georgian symmetry with Arts & Crafts tile ornaments and exposed rafter ends," Hamilton writes. "The Ward house has a large half-timbered oriel rising above the roofline above at least three different kinds of front windows. The Charlot house contrasts a brick first floor (now painted) with dark-shingled upper floor and gables. The only feature these three houses have in common is a first-floor sunporch on the east side of each. Partly because of their small size, these porches reveal Spiering's highly developed sense of three-dimensional design and his attention to detail. In what could have been a routine assemblage of standard parts, Spiering has thought through every architectural element as though for the first time."[7]

Additional elements were important. By the time Spiering took up his profession in St. Louis, architects had begun to address the strictures imposed by the steamy Mississippi Valley climate. As Charles C. Savage points out, the introduction of central heating permitted greater design flexibility. Often, he says, "staircases became insulating buffers to allow rooms maximum exposure along the more desirable orientations."[8] Spiering wrote about this in an article describing possibly his earliest St. Louis residence, 5886 Clemens Avenue, designed in 1905 for James P.

FIG. 10.4 *Spiering-designed residence at 4242 Flora Place. MHS.*

Duncan, assistant treasurer, Buxton & Skinner Stationery (FIG. 10.5). "The stairbay borders on the west party line," he noted, "leaving all the vacant space not occupied by the house on the east side. The advantage of this is twofold. In winter the morning sun enters the dining-room and living-room on the first floor and the principal bedrooms on the second floor. In summer the east side of the house, where the porch and terrace are located, is shaded in the afternoon." (The east side porch is nearly a standard feature of Spiering designs.)

Further, he notes, "on each floor every room but one has southern exposure, a matter of considerable importance in a climate where the prevailing breezes in summer are from the south."[9]

Grand Yet Convivial

Quite a number of Spiering residences face north. Another common thread is the corner lots on which many of his houses are situated, affording him an added degree of freedom that he must have relished. Two of his grandest designs occupy corner lots: #36 Westmoreland Place at Lake Avenue, a yellow brick masterpiece of restrained opulence, designed in 1909 for Louis Werner, president of the Louis Werner Saw Mill Company; and the neo-Tudor #48 Washington Terrace at Clara, built the same year for Leonard B. Hirsch, president of Cal Hirsch & Sons Iron & Rail Company (FIG. 10.6 and FIG. 10.7).

FIG. 10.5 *Spiering-designed residence at 5886 Clemens Avenue. MHS.*

Even these two upper-end residences displayed the Spiering predilection for the asymmetrical, climatically correct design described by Charles C. Savage. It almost appears as if Spiering the architect was improving upon the north-facing row house of his Chambers Street childhood—multiplying and enlarging all the windows, creating side exposure stairwells, usually embellished by stained glass windows at the landings, and east exposure porches. Certainly the St. Louis climate was a factor. Yet a contemporary observer no longer so concerned with temperature control might notice that there's something familial about the off-center plans, undeniably reminiscent of Spiering's childhood household. There's a kind of in-touchness to living in one of these houses—a sense of being connected to other members of the family, even though the traffic patterns are unintrusive, and common rooms offer inglenooks, window seats—what we now call "away spaces."

In suburban Webster Groves, Spiering designed two houses in the sylvan subdivision of Webster Park. For Frederick L. Davis, he created a two-and-a-half-story, clapboard and shingle center hall plan on the level, south-facing lot at 225 Spencer Road (FIG. 10.8). The front of the residence, built in 1911, is so severely symmetrical that one almost doubts its authorship. The sides and rear, however, show Spiering's hand, with abundant cross-ventilation provided by the windowed

gables and setbacks. A large bay window enhances the east
exposure, while the west side gains light and air through a two-
story bump-out in the corner. Here, Spiering has ingeniously
worked two stacked, angled and operable windows directly
into the corner; their convex placement allows the stairwell
to be situated within. (A neat design solution similar to that
achieved at the Davis house on Flora Place.)

Several blocks and seemingly half a world away is
Spiering's project for Theodore Blair, a department manager
for Rice, Stix Dry Goods Company.

In contrast to the flat, gridlike
Spencer Road location, Blair's
site at 115 Glen Road is a long,
wooded hill that terminates in a
creek running parallel to the road.
Responding to the rare opportunity
to design in a quasi-rural setting,
Spiering created a "country" retreat
at the hill's crest that resembles a
Swiss chalet, as Esley Hamilton has
observed.[10] This effect is heightened
by features such as the rustic

balustrade of the porch that runs the full width of the east
(front) exposure (FIG. 10.9). The wood frame Blair house is
still its original dark brown color.

FIG. 10.6 *Spiering-
designed residence at
36 Westmoreland Place.
Photograph by Howard
Porter, 2003.*

"Chinese Puzzle"

How much of Spiering's residential work is of his own
conception, and how much is the result of client pressure?
Was he speaking from experience when he wrote this passage
in 1907?

"The American architect's client is too often of that type
of American citizen who comes out baldly and frankly with
the statement, 'I guess I know what I want, and, besides, I am
paying for this,' or else a person of superficial attainments,
a dilettante nature who attempts to plan his own house,
subscribes to a half dozen architectural journals, copies the
living room from one, the kitchen from another, a closet
from still another, and after concocting a most horrible
conglomeration carries his Chinese puzzle to an architect and
instructs him to make a few working drawings and to have the
design executed."[11]

FIG. 10.7 AND 10.8
*Spiering-designed
residences at 48
Washington Terrace
(top) and 225 Spencer
Road, Webster Groves.
Photographs by
the author, 2000.*

To the extent that Spiering's designs hold together, he appears to have been free of such indignities. And he could be firm. The friend who eulogized Spiering in 1912 put it this way: "Not robust but resolute; practical but with high ideals; gentle but persistent; he was ever arrayed against the cheap, the sham, the merely popular."[12]

Researchers continue to turn up structures credited to Spiering. Of the residences we know he designed, only about half are still standing. Miraculously, another Spiering creation remains for viewing enjoyment: a handsome 70-by-175-foot sunken garden, currently undergoing restoration, at the corner of Waterman and Union in the Central West End. It was designed in 1909 for retailer Sigmund Baer as a birthday gift for Mrs. Baer. The garden adjoined the Baer residence on Waterman, designed earlier by George W. Hellmuth. The east exposure of the Baer house, now an appealing, green-tiled conservatory, appears to have been reworked for that purpose, probably by Spiering, to take full advantage of the adjacent garden and its fountains, walkways and pergola.

"The Beautiful Things of This Life" — Public Buildings

"Art is long but life is short," Louis Spiering wrote in his Christmas message of 1911. "While there is life, may we be blessed with inspiration and enthusiasm reinforced by health and vigor, so that we may contribute our small share to the beautiful things of this life."[13] As a maturing architect, Spiering displayed a talent for designing multi-purpose buildings meant to shelter the visual and performing arts and to promote learning and culture. His first opportunity to cultivate this gift came in the early 1890s, as we have seen, during his employment with William Otis of Chicago as he was pressed

into service on Otis' Evanston project, the Orrington Lunt
Library at Northwestern University.

Such an opportunity next came with the commission to
design the Conservatory at Stephens College in Columbia,
Missouri (FIG. 10.10). Later known as Gauntlett Hall, this
1907 structure, which harmoniously brought together the
activities of music performance and rehearsal, physical
education and college administration, survived on the
Stephens campus until the mid-1990s.

University Methodist Church in Austin, Texas,
completed in 1909, is credited today as the work of
Frederick M. Mann (1868–1959), St. Louis architect and
earliest chair of the architecture program at Washington
University. Yet Spiering routinely included the church in his
list of designs. His claim warrants consideration; he and Mann
had collaborated on at least one other project (their design
won third prize in the 1905 competition for the Missouri
Supreme Court building in Jefferson City)[14] and exceptional
acoustics are to be enjoyed in the church, a Mediterranean-
influenced building of native Texas limestone (FIG. 10.11).
The structure is significant, for it set the style for the adjacent
central campus of University of Texas, laid out in the 1920s
by Philadelphia architect and Beaux-Arts *ancien* Paul Philippe
Cret (1876–1945).[15]

The 1908 St. Louis Artists' Guild clubhouse at 812 Union
Boulevard in the Central West End, another acoustical success,
was an inside job for Spiering. As a member and later an
officer in this organization of vocal and headstrong creative
types, Spiering knew instinctively how to create a fanciful and
altogether functional home for his comperes. He satisfied the
Guild's need for gallery space, provided a cozy rathskeller and
kitchen for their famous "Bohemian dinners," and tucked in a
picturesque upstairs nook for the secret goings-on of the allied
Burns Club, a group of Scots heritage enthusiasts led by the
wealthy St. Louis philanthropist William K. Bixby, benefactor
of Washington University and the St. Louis Art Museum.
The Burns Club had been seeking a home since it formed to
sponsor the Burns Cottage at the St. Louis World's Fair.

In the early 1970s, the Artists' Guild moved its
headquarters to suburban Webster Groves, and ultimately to

FIG. 10.9 *Detail from
entry banister, 115 Glen
Road. Photograph by the
author, 2000.*

FIG. 10.10 *Conservatory (later Gauntlett Hall) at Stephens College, Columbia, Mo. Drawing by Louis Spiering. Stephensophia. Stephens College Archives.*

Clayton, site of its current home at Oak Knoll Park. The Spiering building on Union Boulevard was purchased by the United Church of Christ in 1975, and serves as the home of Dignity House, an arts enrichment program for neighborhood children.

The clubhouse may be Spiering's most intriguing and skillful statement. The structure has changed hands, suffered the ravages of time and has been altered sensitively and otherwise during its ninety-five years on Union Boulevard. But if we know anything about the early Guild and its determinedly eccentric membership, we can walk in today and see how adroitly Spiering worked out his solutions. The building is a testament to rational Beaux-Arts principles, embodied in an appealing red brick Arts and Crafts cottage, decorated on the exterior with green glazed brick and a subtly wrought frieze of artists' palettes (FIG. 10.12).

A speech at the clubhouse dedication exercises shows Spiering at his most relaxed, as he kidded his colleagues and offered rare commentary on the appearance of his work: "Many questions have been put to me, pertaining to this cottage structure. Why the north side is not as decorative as the south side, why I used a paving brick, why green enameled brick, why the palettes, why they are brown, why the ladies' coat room doesn't house a lounge and many other whys.

I believe to have had a reason for most of these whys if not for all of them.

If my reasons were not legitimate I beg to express my regret, for it was certainly my earnest desire to please the majority of my Fellow Guilders and not to antagonize them aesthetically in any way."[16]

Library Design Provokes Conflict

Louis Spiering's penultimate public building was the Soulard branch of the St. Louis Public Library, 708 Lafayette Avenue, dedicated in March 1910. He designed the Andrew Carnegie-funded library during his brief partnership with George W. Hellmuth. When Spiering's library design (FIG.

10.13) won the competition and went on display with the rest of the 21 entries, a dozen of his competitors raised a protest, claiming that Spiering had violated the competition rule restricting architects to the use of a single medium—India ink—in their entries. The protesters also claimed that he had exceeded the limit of 210,000 cubic feet.

Spiering replied that he had followed all the rules, including the one governing the use of media, and stated that the measurements of his drawing provided for a building of 208,000 cubic feet.[17] As l'affaire Soulard came to a boil, Spiering dutifully pasted all the attendant press coverage into his scrapbook. The library board dismissed the protest, and work on the building went forward. It is possible that Spiering's exquisite Beaux-Arts drafting technique was responsible for the deceptive subtleties he achieved within a single medium. The Soulard building was decommissioned by the public library system in 1962; it later became home to the Phoenix Musical Club and then to a succession of restaurants. In 2003, it stands vacant.

FIG. 10.11 *University Methodist Church, Austin, Texas. Austin History Center.*

The Sheldon Memorial

"Have you seen the plans for our new building? I like the ideas very well," wrote one Ethical Society officer in 1910.[18]

The ideas, of course, were those of Louis Spiering, whose appointment had been a condition of Anna Hartshorne Sheldon's $37,000 challenge grant to the organization's building fund. Spiering accepted the commission in mid-February 1910, and within a month had produced plans for the new home of the Ethical Society of St. Louis. Established in 1886, the society was—and remains—a nondenominational organization committed to the betterment of self and society through ethical behavior. It is affiliated with the American Ethical Union. As a subscribing member of the St. Louis society, Spiering again brought an insider's insight to his design along with his talent for creating multi-use facilities (FIG. 10.14).

FIG. 10.12 *St. Louis Artists' Guild Clubhouse, 812 North Union. MHS.*

FIG. 10.13 *Soulard Branch Library, 706 Lafayette. Drawing by Louis Spiering. MHS.*

The plans called for a 760-seat auditorium with balcony; an additional large, multi-purpose skylit assembly area with stage; kitchen facilities; various smaller meeting rooms; a handsome library with fireplace; and an office for the society leader, all wrapped in an elegantly simple classical revival package and bearing an estimated price tag of $75,000. (Final cost of the structure, however, exceeded $100,000.)

Spiering also had the professional expertise to include a feature not immediately apparent in any drawing or blueprint: acoustical purity. Working at the Louisiana Purchase Exposition, he had witnessed dramatic public failures of acoustics on the fairgrounds; both the Palace of Liberal Arts and Festival Hall required extensive corrections before they could be used. Spiering wanted to build an auditorium that would do honor to the philosophical discourse and exemplary music that lay at the heart of the society's Sunday morning meetings, called "platforms." In June 1910, Spiering obtained the consultation of Wallace Clement Sabine, Harvard physicist and acoustical consultant for the Boston Symphony Hall, whose pioneering research later earned him the title "Father of Modern Acoustics." The Spiering-Sabine collaboration ensured the Sheldon Memorial lasting acclaim as an acoustical treasure.

Enthusiasm for the new meeting house ran high, and not just among Society members. The *St. Louis Globe-Democrat* hailed the Sheldon Memorial as "a thing sadly needed in the city," and predicted: "This will be a gathering place for the intellectual life of the town."[19]

But as the new building rose on Washington Boulevard, the health of its creator declined. Louis Spiering's first signs of illness appeared in the summer of 1910. During the next twenty months, he underwent three surgeries for intestinal cancer and lengthy convalescences in St. Louis and Asheville, North Carolina. Spiering eventually resigned from his Washington University faculty position, and from a prestigious appointment as architectural advisor to the Missouri State

Capitol Commission Board
— all in hope of marshaling his
energy for the completion of the
Sheldon Memorial.

Spiering carried out
his supervisory duties until
the end, literally from his
deathbed, signing checks to
subcontractors hours before he
lapsed into a coma from which
he did not rally. Louis Spiering
died March 9, 1912, two
months before his 38th birthday.
The Sheldon Memorial was dedicated the following October.

Fɪɢ. 10.14 *The Sheldon Memorial. Drawing by Humphry Woolrych. MHS.*

＊　　　＊　　　＊

In 1907, Louis Spiering wrote: "A good design must
first of all solve the specific problem in regard to its practical
requirements, meet the prescribed needs of usefulness, must
be adapted to the climate, the nature of the ground, the points
of compass, must be convenient, economical and beautiful."
He added: "A style is only a living style so long as it gives
expression to the feeling of the time, and the outward form it
takes results from its more or less complete expression of this
feeling."[20]

In many ways, the mission of an early twentieth century
exposition architect was to turn these principles inside out.
Working hastily and in ignorance of interior requirements or
even compass points in many cases, architects were charged
to create elaborate, expensive facades meant to last no longer
than six months. "Beautiful," the last criterion on Spiering's
list, was the first consideration at the fair.

Louis Spiering's exposition work shows his adaptability;
where the Main Picture was concerned, he fell in with the
illusion, he willingly suspended disbelief. But he refused to
be enslaved by tradition, and his smaller structures did give
"expression to the feeling of the time"—the new time just ahead
that he anticipated, embraced, but did not live to see.

Epilogue

January 25, 1905

Louis Spiering unlocked the door to his office, turned on the light and stepped inside. He raised the shades, and eastern sun poured in to warm the chilly room.

Something about the surroundings seemed slightly amiss, though Louis had taken time last week to neaten the place before leaving for the train station.

Approaching his desk, he noticed that Hellmuth, entrusted with a key, had been up to collect the mail. Was there anything in it that demanded his immediate attention? Louis leaned on a corner of the desk and began to leaf through the envelopes. A telephone bill. Confirmation of his lecture series just six weeks away. Would Mr. Spiering be using lantern slides? Concert tickets. A notice of the first smoker of the semester, to be held downstairs at Lippe's. Louis smiled. His students were building an esprit de corps worthy of the rowdiest Beaux-Arts atelier. By spring, they would launch the first university architectural club. Rumor had it they were even composing their own song.

And his evening students, draftsmen from throughout the city, were coming along splendidly on sketch problems, and even on the competitions issued by the Society of Beaux-Arts Architects.

What else? A notice of the February AIA meeting. Louis had promised a summary of his observations at the Washington national convention. One of the choicest bits he would have to keep to himself for now: Masqueray was almost certain to receive the commission for the new Cathedral of St. Paul, he had confided to Louis at the welcoming reception. Archbishop John Ireland had met him last year at the fair when he traveled down from Minnesota—Louis remembered the meeting—and had been instantly enamored of Masqueray's ideas.

Ah, Louis thought, things are looking up. At last, a letter from Duncan, commenting on recent amendments to the residence on Clemens Avenue. Finally, it appeared, Duncan recognized the wisdom of orienting the house to suit St. Louis' beastly climate. And if he still had qualms, they would disappear after he had lived one summer in a house that provided adequate exposure to the prevailing southern breezes. Elementary, really. Why should it even be open to question?

Here was a note from Aunt Thekla, extolling the virtues of the Ethical Society, with an enclosure: notice of the latest address by Professor Sheldon. And a note from Uncle August, urging Louis to resist the bamboozlings of Thek, and to concentrate on more practical matters, such as the clinic he hoped to build. When could they meet to discuss designs? A message from Moss confirmed what Louis had suspected: the poor fellow was hopelessly besotted with Vida Gruner. Well, much happiness to them. Romance to Louis seemed a distant impossibility, something painful to be avoided at all costs. Admittedly, he had noticed a certain flurry among the groups of female university students when they passed him on campus. More than once, on these occasions, he had heard soprano voices trilling "Meet Me in St. Louis, Louis" when the gaggle was nearly out of range. That blasted song. At least 1905 would see an end to it!

The fair now seemed to Louis as distant and impossible as his memories of Sigrid. And he realized what it was that had given him pause when he entered the office. Swinging around, he stared at the wall behind his desk, filled with imagery of the fair. Beneath his handsomely framed diploma was tacked a rough schematic drawing of Art Hill, with festival buildings, cascades and landscaped walkways sketched in. To the right of the drawing was a photograph of the restaurant pavilion. Louis remembered Aunt Thekla's reaction when word of the Fair City Club takeover of the pavilion had made its way into the newspapers. She was always ready with an epigram from her beloved Goethe. "The fate of the architect," she had quoted sardonically, "is the strangest of all. How often he expends his whole soul, his whole heart and passion, to produce buildings into which he himself may never enter."

Beneath the pavilion, on Louis' World's Fair wall, reposed his perspective drawing of the Palais du Costume. What a lovely building he had created for the exhibit. Lovely and at long last emptied of its displays, a shell awaiting the wrecking crew.

Now Louis began to pry at one of the tacks holding the Palais drawing in place. As recently as last week, he realized, he had been so accustomed to the sight of these images that he took their presence for granted. But the gatherings in Philadelphia and Washington had freshened his perspective. It was 1905 now. The fair was over, new projects were in the works, and Louis would need the wall space to display his sketches. It was time to clear away that which had passed, time to make room for the new.

Notes

Chapter One *Growing Up on Chambers Street*

1. Wilma Guyot, conversation, March 1999.

2. *Der Deutsche Pioneer,* article trans. Lenore Spiering. (Cincinnati: March 1880.) Typewritten copy, private collection of Wilma Guyot.

3. Henry Boernstein, *Memoirs of a Nobody: The Missouri Years of an Austrian Radical, 1849–1866,* trans. Steven Rowan (St. Louis: Missouri Historical Society Press, 1997), p. 9.

4. Ibid, p. 13.

5. Thekla Bernays, *Augustus Charles Bernays: A Memoir* (St. Louis: C.V. Mosby Co., 1912), p. 105.

6. see Larry Tye, *The Father of Spin: Edward L. Bernays & the Birth of Public Relations* (New York: Crown Publishers, 1998).

7. So said Helmut Hirsch, author of *Freund von Heine, Marx/Engels und Lincoln: Eine Karl Ludwig Bernays–Biographie* (Frankfurt am Main: Peter Lang GmbH, 2002), in correspondence, October 25, 2000.

8. Thekla Bernays, *A.C. Bernays,* p. 122.

9. Willard Bartlett, M.D., F.A.C.S., "Augustus Charles Bernays," Bernays Collection, MHS.

10. *St. Louis Globe-Democrat,* July 30, 1901. Bernays was actually warning against sporadic exertion by otherwise sedentary men.

11. *Missouri Republican,* 1887. Sarah B. Hull Scrapbook, p. 16, MHS.

12. W. A. Kelsoe, *St. Louis Reference Record: A Newspaper Man's Motion-Picture of the City When We Got our First Bridge, and of Many Later Happenings of Local Note* (St. Louis: Von Hoffmann Press: 1927), p. 94.

13. $70,000, according to his granddaughter, Wilma Guyot. Conversation, March 1999.

Chapter Two *The Chicago Years*

1. William A. Otis, lecture notes, Winnetka Historical Society.

2. Ibid.

3. Richard Guy Wilson, *The American Renaissance, 1876–1917* (Brooklyn: The Brooklyn Museum, 1979), pp. 87–88.

4. Letter from LCS to Theresa Bernays Spiering, April 4, 1902. Collection of the author.

5. Northwestern University Archives.

6. William A. Otis, "The Orrington Lunt Library: the Building Architecturally," *The Northwestern,* Sept. 21, 1894, p. 4.

7. Ibid.

8. Ibid.

9. William A. Otis to Dr. R. D. Sheppard, Nov. 3, 1893, Northwestern University Archives.

10. *Dictionary of American Biography* (New York: Charles Scribner's Sons, 1935), pp. 457–458.

Chapter Three *Seven Years in Paris*

1. Isabelle Gournay, *Le Voyage de Paris*, p. 47.

2. Chafee, p. 82.

3. Louis Sullivan to Albert Sullivan, quoted by Willard Connely in "Louis Sullivan as He Lived," New York, 1960, p. 62. Cited by Chafee, p. 90.

4. Louis C. Spiering, "American Schools of Architecture," *The Architectural Record*, Nov. 1907, p. 393. Publications, 1956), p. 240.

5. Esley Hamilton, "Louis Clemens Spiering: St. Louis Architect," exhibit display text, The Sheldon Art Galleries, September 1999.

6. Louis Henri Sullivan, *The Autobiography of an Idea.* (New York: Dover Publications, 1956), p. 240.

7. Hugh Ferriss, *Power in Buildings: An Artist's View of Contemporary Architecture* (New York: Columbia University, 1956), p. 6.

8. By the post-World War II years they were the accepted norm.

9. "The Charrette [sic]," *Student Life,* May 10, 1911, page 3.

10. Letter from LCS to Theresa Spiering, October 22, 1899. Collection of the author. Spiering's letters were written in German; the author is indebted to Steven Rowan for his spirited translations.

11. Wilma Guyot, conversation, March 1999.

12. An apparent trick question translated from Spiering's original quotation in French and explained to the author by Roland Champagne.

13. LCS to TS, October 22, 1899. Collection of the author.

14. LCS to TS, April 4, 1902. Collection of the author.

15. LCS to TS, March 21, 1900. Collection of the author.

16. George Julian Zolnay, *Illustrated Handbook of the Missouri Art Exhibit,* p. 55. This catalog describes the works of art represented in the art gallery of the Missouri State Building in the 1905 Lewis and Clark Exposition, Portland, Ore. In October 1905, a fire devastated the Missouri building and destroyed its contents.

17. Letter from Richard Chafee to the author, March 22, 2001.

Chapter Four *Making Magic—The Design Staff*

1. Louis LaBeaume, "Looking Backward at St. Louis Architecture," *Missouri Historical Society Bulletin*, January 1958, p. 187.

2. Two typewritten captions in the album probably were added decades later by Spiering's niece Lenore.

3. Louisiana Purchase Exposition Scrapbook, Vol. 123. Masqueray was remembered as not altogether fluent in spoken English. He could have been assisted in the composition of this essay by Isaac Taylor, or by any number of newspaper reporters and editors who worked for the LPE Company. Another possibility is that Louis Spiering translated Masqueray's original from French to English.

4. Ibid.

5. Time and Salary Report, LPE Co. Collection, MHS. LCS was one of three "draftsmen" to earn this figure, equivalent to $4,000+ per month in today's economy, according to the Bureau of Labor Statistics. The only higher salaries were $216.66, $208 and $200 per month. The time and salary report for the architectural department filed August 1, 1904 names a total of 67 employees on staff at various times throughout 1901–1904. An earlier document lists 84 "draughtsmen."

6. LaBeaume, p. 186.

7. An almost pathological modesty governed the public personae of Louis Spiering and his gifted musician brother, Theodore. In 1911, a music journalist speculated that Theodore Spiering, then concertmaster for the New York Philharmonic Orchestra, had been passed over for the conductorship vacated by Gustav Mahler because he was "too modest and too honest to pull the wires." [See news clipping, Theodore Spiering Scrapbook, Vol. I, pp. 174-175, Chicago Historical Society.] in 1921, Theodore Spiering vied unsuccessfully for the position of music director of the St. Louis Symphony Orchestra. In 1925, he was named conductor of the Portland (Oregon) Symphony Orchestra. He died of cancer later that year, a month before the beginning of the fall season.

8. Louis C. Spiering, to Mrs. Walter Sheldon, February 5, 1910, WHMC. Anna Sheldon subsequently commissioned Spiering architect of the new home to be built for the Ethical Society of St. Louis.

9. LaBeaume, pp. 185-186.

10. Ibid. Swales, however, in his own later essays remembers Masqueray affectionately and with a high degree of professional admiration. See "Master Draftsman VII: Emmanuel Louis Masqueray 1862-1917," *Pencil Points*, 5:65, November 1924.

11. David R. Francis to Miss Caroline Weber, November 15, 1902, MHS.

12. *World's Fair Bulletin*, February 1904, p. 44.

13. Executive Committee Minutes, LPE Co., January 19, 1904, MHS.

14. Bertha Skinker to Thomas Skinker, July 6, 1901; Thomas Skinker to "My Dear Wife," July 16, 1901, Thomas S. Skinker Papers, MHS.

15. Anne Johnson [Mrs. Charles P.], *Notable Women of St. Louis*. (St. Louis: Woodward, 1914), p. 23.

16. *St. Louis Globe-Democrat*, August 10, 1902.

Chapter Five *"A Magnificent View" — The West Restaurant Pavilion*

1. Emmanuel Masqueray, Louisiana Purchase Exposition Scrapbook, Vol. 123, MHS.

2. Gilbert's Central Public Library in downtown St. Louis, completed in 1912, was his second contribution of Beaux-Arts design to the 1904 World's Fair city.

3. Pamela Gayle Hemenway, *Cass Gilbert's Buildings at the Louisiana Purchase Exposition, 1904* (Master's thesis, University of Missouri, 1970), p. 18.

4. Ibid, pp. 38-39.

5. *St. Louis Globe-Democrat*, January 24, 1904.

6. Robert W. Rydell, *All the World's a Fair: Visions of Empire at American International Expositions* (Chicago and London: University of Chicago Press, 1984), p. 136.

7. Frederick M. Mann, "Architecture at the Exposition," *The Bulletin of the Washington University Association*, April 23, 1904.

8. George Julian Zolnay, "Illustrated Handbook of the Missouri Art Exhibit" (St. Louis: Saint Louis Artists' Guild, 1905), p. 55.

9. Masqueray, op. cit.

10. "World's Fair Authentic Guide: A Complete Reference Book to St. Louis and the Louisiana Purchase Exposition." (St. Louis: The Official Guide Company, 1904), pp. 32-33.

11. Sara Jane Rorer held the restaurant concession contract for the East Restaurant Pavilion.

12. Minutes of the Executive Committee, LPE Co., December 7, 1902, MHS.

13. Ibid.

14. Ibid.

15. *St. Louis Globe-Democrat,* April 13, 1904.

16. Minutes of the Grounds & Buildings Committee, LPE Co. April 18, 1904, MHS.

17. Minutes of the Executive Committee, LPE Co., April 23, 1904, MHS.

18. Ibid., p. 2554.

19. David R .Francis, *The Universal Exposition of 1904, Volume I* (St. Louis: Louisiana Purchase Exposition Company, 1913), p. 214.

Chapter Six *Old and New—The French and Austrian Pavilions*

1. *St. Louis Globe-Democrat,* January 3, 1903.

2. James Neal Primm, *Lion of the Valley: St. Louis, Missouri 1764-1980,* 3rd ed. (St. Louis: Missouri Historical Society Press, 1998), p. 386.

3. Marcel Lambert, calling card, private collection. Translated by Marilyn Maguire.

4. *The Mirror,* April 4, 1904.

5. *Globe-Democrat,* January 14, 1904.

6. *Globe-Democrat,* March 5, 1904.

7. *Globe-Democrat,* November 29, 1903.

8. *World's Fair Bulletin,* July 1904, p. 30.

9. *Globe-Democrat,* March 22, 1903.

10. *WFB*, November, 1901, p. 5.

11. *The Austrian Government Pavilion*, brochure, Department of Rare Books and Special Collections, St. Louis Public Library.

12. *WFB*, June 1904, p. 26. In this article, the WFB incorrectly refers to the Vienna Artists' Association as the "Vienna Artists Society."

13. *Globe-Democrat*, June 3, 1904.

14. *Globe-Democrat*, April 15, 1904.

Chapter Seven *The Express Office—Spiering and the 'Little Buildings'*

1. Robert Duffy, interview, February 7, 2002.

2. *St. Louis Globe-Democrat*, August 22, 1903.

3. Ibid.

4. Presumably August A. Busch, Sr.

5. Minutes of the Grounds & Buildings Committee, LPE Co. March 12, 1904.

6. Ibid, April 12, 1904.

7. Osmund Overby, interview, March 11, 2003.

8. Minutes of the Executive Committee, LPE Co., September 19, 2002.

9. *World's Fair Bulletin*, March 1902, p. 31.

10. Duffy, ibid. Portland Place is a World's-Fair era private street in the Central West End, an enclave of palatial residences owned by many of the city's upper class.

11. *Globe-Democrat*, May 9, 1903.

12. Esley Hamilton, interview, Nov. 12, 2001.

13. A few years later, LaBeaume did include a TPA building design with examples of his work, when applying for membership in the American Institute of Architects, St. Louis Chapter. Unfortunately, no record remains to tell us which design he submitted.

14. *Globe-Democrat*, June 11, 1904.

Chapter Eight *The Palais on the Pike*

1. *Palais du Costume,* brochure, St. Louis Public Library, Department of Rare Books and Special Collections.

2. *The Greatest of Expositions* (St. Louis: Louisiana Purchase Exposition Company, 1904), p. 266.

3. The concept of the period room would make another appearance in Forest Park, courtesy of Louis LaBeaume. As a twenty-five-year member of the Saint Louis Art Museum Board of Directors, and for ten years (1931–41) its president, LaBeaume guided the museum in the installation of medieval galleries and European and American rooms. These period rooms, though popular with the public, assembled antique furniture and objects into "poorly faked ensembles," wrote Osmund Overby in his 1987 architectural history of the museum, and were discontinued after "the closer scrutiny of modern curatorial study" sent the museum in other directions.

4. Minutes, LPE Company Executive Committee, May 12, 1903 and October 1, 1903. President of the Palais du Costume Company was Charles R. Blake, president, Sligo Iron Store Company.

5. *World's Fair Bulletin,* November 1903, p. 36.

6. Osmund Overby, interview, March 17, 2003.

7. *The Greatest of Expositions,* p. 26.

8. *WFB,* April 1904, p. 66. John Carson and Harry F. Hudson formed this alliance with W.H.H. Weatherwax, chief draftsman in the LPE architectural department. They had done similar work at the Buffalo exposition.

9. Minutes of the Executive Committee, LPE Co., October 18, 1904.

10. "Creation" was shipped to Coney Island and installed in the Dreamland amusement park.

Chapter Nine *Up in Lights — The American De Forest Wireless Telegraph Tower*

1. Susan J. Douglas, *Inventing American Broadcasting: 1899–1922* (Baltimore: The Johns Hopkins University Press, 1987), p. 48.

2. Douglas, p. 40.

3. Samuel Lubell, "Magnificent Failure," The Saturday Evening Post, January 24, 1942, p. 41.

4. Lee De Forest, quoted by Tom Lewis in *Empire of the Air—The Men Who Made Radio* (New York: HarperCollins, 1991), p. 42.

5. Douglas, p. 92.

6. Lee De Forest, *Father of Radio—The Autobiography of Lee de Forest* (Chicago: Wilcox & Follett Co., 1950), p. 63.

7. *St. Louis Globe-Democrat*, September 8, 1903.

8. Douglas, p. 97.

9. Isaac Taylor, "Report on Percentage of Completion of Buildings," cited in LPE Company Executive Committee Minutes, Dec. 7, 1903, MHS.

10. Minutes of the Executive Committee, LPE Co., February 23, 1904.

11. *The Mirror*, April 21, 1910.

12. *St. Louis Post-Dispatch*, September 13, 1904.

13. Mark Bennitt, *History of the Louisiana Purchase Exposition*, (St. Louis: Universal Exposition Publishing Company, 1905), p. 623.

14. *Post-Dispatch*, op. cit.

15. Minutes of the Executive Committee, LPE Co., January 9, 1905, MHS.

16. *Globe-Democrat*, December 24, 1904.

17. Ibid., December 15, 1904.

18. Gloria Dalton, ed., *Heritage of the Creve Coeur Area* (City of Creve Coeur, Mo.: 1976), pp. 151–152. The tower was demolished in 1934.

19. Lewis, *Empire of the Air,* pp. 49–52.

20. Ibid.

Chapter Ten *1904 and Beyond*

1. Holmes Smith, funeral address for Louis Clemens Spiering, March 11, 1912.

2. Gilbert's Art Palace won the exposition's gold medal in architecture. The only additional St. Louis firms exhibiting were: Barnett, Haynes & Barnett, Eames & Young, Theodore Link, Montrose P. McArdle, Mauran, Russell & Garden, Samuel L. Sherer and Isaac Taylor.

3. George McCue, "Cass Gilbert: Eminence, Oblivion And Now Renewed Appreciation." *St. Louis Post-Dispatch,* April 13, 1975.

4. The market for Secession architecture was limited. Only a handful of such residences remain in St. Louis as witness to the interest of some local architects and a very few adventuresome clients. William Hirsch, Spiering's collaborator on the Palais du Costume, built a house for himself at 6236 Waterman Place. in 1908 that suggests Secessionist influence. The exotic #17 Hortense Place., significantly "modernized" by the last quarter of the twentieth century, but still a wonder to behold, was designed by Tom Barnett in 1909 for J. W. Thompson. Barnett's own Maryland Avenue residence, a frank Secessionist statement circa 1908–1909, burned in 1973. See Savage, (*Private Streets*).

5. Hellmuth was the father of George F. Hellmuth, cofounder of the present-day architectural firm Hellmuth, Obata + Kassabaum.

6. Julius K. Hunter, *Kingsbury Place—The First Two Hundred Years*, pp. 75 and 84.

7. Esley Hamilton, "Louis Clemens Spiering: St. Louis Architect," The Sheldon Art Galleries, September, 1999.

8. Charles C. Savage, *Architecture of the Private Streets of St. Louis,* p. 222.

9. "A Residence for Mr. James P. Duncan, St. Louis," pp. 172-3. This unbylined article, most likely written by Louis Spiering, is among his papers at the Missouri Historical Society. The clipping is not labeled with title of publication or date.

10. Hamilton, op. cit.

11. Louis Clemens Spiering, "American Schools of Architecture," *The Architectural Record,* November, 1907, p. 388.

12. Smith, op.cit.

13. LCS, Christmas card, December, 1911.

14. Competition winners were Mariner & LaBeaume.

15. There is every probability of Cret-Mann-Spiering connections. Cret and Spiering attended the Ecole contemporaneously. From there, Cret went to Philadelphia as a professor of design in the department of architecture at University of Pennsylvania—joining the faculty that Mann had just left to head the architecture program at Washington University in St. Louis. Spiering's acquaintance with Cret and Mann may have been the connection that led him to participate in the Philadelphia T-Square Club exhibition of 1904. His contribution was a design for a courthouse in Columbia County, Arkansas.

16. LCS, speech to members of the St. Louis Artists' Guild, February 11, 1908. MHS.

17. "Library Board Stands By Its Decisions," *St. Louis Post-Dispatch*, June 23, 1908.

18. Joseph L. Taussig, "Dear Mr. Herzog," ALS, March 16, 1910. Archives of the Ethical Society of St. Louis. (HQ)

19. "Ethical Culture Society Plans Greek Building to Cost $100,000," *St. Louis Globe-Democrat*, December 18, 1910.

20. LCS, *The Architectural Record*, November, 1907, p. 392.

Bibliography

Books and Articles

The American Renaissance: 1876–1917. With essays Richard Guy Wilson, Dianne Pilgrim, and Richard N. Murray. Brooklyn: The Brooklyn Museum, 1979.

Barnes, Harper. *Standing on a Volcano: The Life and Times of David Rowland Francis*. St. Louis: Missouri Historical Society Press, 2001.

Bartlett, Willard, M.D., F.A.C.S., "Augustus Charles Bernays," *Journal of Surgery, Gynecology and Obstetrics*, February 1, 1937.

Bennitt, Mark. *History of the Louisiana Purchase Exposition*. St. Louis: Universal Exposition Publishing Company, 1905.

Bernays, Thekla. *Augustus Charles Bernays: A Memoir*. St. Louis: C. V. Mosby Company, 1912.

Boernstein, Henry. *Memoirs of a Nobody: The Missouri Years of an Austrian Radical, 1849–1866*. Translated and edited by Steven Rowan. St. Louis: Missouri Historical Society Press, 1997.

Bryan, John Albury. *Missouri's Contribution to American Architecture*. St. Louis: St. Louis Architectural Club, 1928.

"The Charrette" [sic], *Student Life,* May 10, 1911.

Clevenger, Martha R. *'Indescribably Grand': Diaries and Letters from the 1904 World's Fair*. St. Louis: Missouri Historical Society Press, 1996.

Dalton, Gloria, ed. *Heritage of the Creve Coeur Area*. City of Creve Coeur: 1976.

De Forest, Lee. *Father of Radio: The Autobiography of Lee de Forest*. Chicago: Wilcox & Follett, 1950.

Douglas, Susan J. *Inventing American Broadcasting: 1899–1922*. Baltimore: The Johns Hopkins University Press, 1987.

Drexler, Arthur, ed. *The Architecture of the Ecole des Beaux-Arts*. Essays by Richard Chafee, Arthur Drexler, Neil Levine, David Van Zanten. The Museum of Modern Art, New York. Distributed by The MIT Press, Cambridge: 1977.

Evenson, Norma. *Paris: A Century of Change, 1878–1978*. New Haven: Yale University Press, 1979.

Eksteins, Modris. *Rites of Spring: The Great War and the Birth of the Modern Age*. New York: Houghton-Mifflin, 1989.

Ferriss, Hugh. *Power in Buildings: An Artist's View of Contemporary Architecture*. New York: Columbia University Press, 1953.

Fox, Timothy J. and Duane R. Sneddeker. *From the Palaces to the Pike: Visions of the 1904 World's Fair*. St. Louis: Missouri Historical Society, 1997.

Francis, David R. *The Universal Exposition of 1904*. 2 vols., St. Louis: Louisiana Purchase Exposition Company, 1913.

The Greatest of Expositions: Completely Illustrated. St. Louis: The Louisiana Purchase Exposition Company, 1904.

Greenhalgh, Paul, ed. *Art Nouveau, 1890–1914.* London: V & A Publications, 2000.

Greenhalgh, Paul. *Ephemeral Vistas: The Expositions Universelles, Great Exhibitions and World's Fairs, 1851–1939.* Manchester: Manchester University Press, 1988.

Gournay, Isabelle in *Le Voyage de Paris: Les Americains dans les ecoles d'art 1868–1918.* With Paris: Editions de la Reunion des musees nationaux, 1990.

Hansen, Eric C. *The Cathedral of Saint Paul: An Architectural Biography.* Saint Paul: The Cathedral of Saint Paul, Saint Paul, 1990.

Harris, Neil, Wim de Wit, James Gilbert and Robert W. Rydell. *Grand Illusions: Chicago World's Fair of 1893.* Chicago: Chicago Historical Society, 1993.

Hoft, Brigitte. *"Mein lieber Spiering": Musikerbriefe aus zwei Kontinenten.* Mannheim: Palatium Verlag, 1996.

Hunter, Julius K. *Kingsbury Place: The First Two Hundred Years.* St. Louis: The C. V. Mosby Company, 1982.

Hunter, Julius K. *Westmoreland and Portland Places: The History and Architecture of America's Premier Private Streets, 1888–1988.* Foreword by James Neal Primm. Essay on the architecture by Esley Hamilton. Columbia: University of Missouri Press, 1988.

Johns, Orrick. *Time of Our Lives: The Story of My Father and Myself.* New York: Stackpole Sons, 1937.

Johnson, Anne. (Mrs. Charles P.) *Notable Women of St. Louis.* St. Louis: Woodward, 1914.

J. J. Jusserand. *What Me Befell: The Reminiscences of J. J. Jusserand.* Boston and New York: Houghton Mifflin Company, 1933.

Kallir, Jane. *Viennese Design and the Wiener Werkstatte.* New York: Galerie St. Etienne/George Braziller, 1986.

LaBeaume, Louis. "Looking Backward at St. Louis Architecture," *Missouri Historical Society Bulletin,* January 1958.

Lewis, Tom. *Empire of the Air: The Men Who Made Radio.* New York: HarperCollins, 1991.

Lubell, Samuel. "Magnificent Failure," *The Saturday Evening Post,* January 24, 1942.

Mandell, Richard D. *Paris 1900: The Great World's Fair.* Toronto: University of Toronto Press, 1967.

Mann, Frederick. "Architecture at the Exposition," *Bulletin of the Washington University Association,* 1904.

McCue, George. "Cass Gilbert: Eminence, Oblivion And Now Renewed Appreciation," *St. Louis Post-Dispatch,* April 13, 1975.

Morrow, Ralph E. *Washington University in St. Louis: A History.* St. Louis: Missouri Historical Society, 1996.

Otis, William A. "The Orrington Lunt Library: the Building Architecturally," *The Northwestern,* September 21, 1894.

Overby, Osmund. "The Saint Louis Art Museum: An Architectural History." St. Louis: *The Bulletin of the Saint Louis Art Museum,* Fall, 1987.

Pevsner, Nikolaus. *Pioneers of the Modern Movement From William Morris to Walter Gropius.* London: Faber & Faber, 1936.

Pridmore, Jay. *Northwestern University: Celebrating 150 Years.* Evanston: Northwestern University Press, 2000.

Primm, James Neal. *Lion of the Valley: St. Louis, Missouri, 1764–1980.* 3rd ed. St. Louis: Missouri Historical Society Press, 1998.

Putzel, Max. *The Man in the Mirror: William Marion Reedy and His Magazine.* Cambridge: Harvard University Press, 1963.

Raguenet, A. *Les Principaux Palais de l'Exposition Universelle de Paris.* Berlin, New York: B. Hessling, 1900.

Rowan, Steven and Primm, James Neal. *Germans for a Free Missouri: Translations from the St. Louis Radical Press, 1857–1862.* Columbia: University of Missouri Press, 1983.

Rydell, Robert W. *All the World's a Fair: Visions of Empire at American International Expositions.* Chicago and London: University of Chicago Press, 1984.

Savage, Charles. *Architecture of the Private Streets of St. Louis.* Columbia: University of Missouri Press, 1987.

Spiering, Louis C. "American Schools of Architecture," *The Architectural Record,* November 1907.

Stein, Susan R., editor. *The Architecture of Richard Morris Hunt.* Chicago and London:University of Chicago Press, 1986.

Sullivan, Louis Henri. *The Autobiography of an Idea.* New York: Dover Publications, 1956.

Swales, Francis. "Master Draftsman VII: Emmanuel Louis Masqueray 1862–1917," *Pencil Points,* November 1924.

Toft, Carolyn Hewes and Jane Molloy Porter. *Compton Heights: A History and Architectural Guide.* St. Louis: Landmarks Association of St. Louis, Inc., 1984.

Toft, Carolyn Hewes. *St. Louis: Landmarks & Historic Districts.* With Lynn Josse. St. Louis: Landmarks Association of St. Louis, Inc., 2002.

Toft, Carolyn Hewes; Esley Hamilton and Mary Henderson Gass. *The Way We Came: A Century of the AIA in St. Louis.* Edited by George McCue. St. Louis: St. Louis Chapter, published by The Patrice Press, 1991.

Toth, Emily. *Kate Chopin: A Life of the Author of "The Awakening."* New York: William Morrow, 1990.

Tye, Larry. *The Father of Spin: Edward L. Bernays & the Birth of Public Relations.* New York: Crown Publishers, 1998.

Interviews and Correspondence

Richard Chafee

Marie-Laure Crosnier Leconte

Robert Duffy

Wilma Guyot

Esley Hamilton

Helmut Hirsch

Jean Ferriss Leich

George McCue

Osmund Overby

Carolyn Toft

Cynthia Weese

Catalogs, Guidebooks, Pamphlets and Reports

(Housed in Rare Books & Special Collections, St. Louis Public Library, unless otherwise noted.)

The Austrian Government Pavilion: Louisiana Purchase Exposition, St. Louis, 1904. Described by Order of the Imp. Royal Ministry of Commerce.

The De Forest Wireless Telegraph System. American De Forest Wireless Telegraph Co.

A Free Souvenir and Correct Map of the Location of All the World's Fair Buildings and of the Features Along 'The Pike.' St. Louis: Mercantile Trust Co., 1904.

Official Guide to the Louisiana Purchase Exposition. Issued by Authority of the Louisiana Purchase Exposition. St. Louis: The Official Guide Co., 1904.

Palais du Costume.

World's Fair Authentic Guide: A Complete Reference Book to St. Louis and the Louisiana Purchase Exposition. St. Louis: The Official Guide Company, 1904.

Zolnay, George Julian. *Illustrated Handbook of the Missouri Art Exhibit: Art Gallery of the Missouri State Building, Lewis and Clark Exposition, Portland Oregon, 1905.* St. Louis: Saint Louis Artists' Guild, 1905. (Saint Louis Art Museum)

Unpublished Material

(Housed in Missouri Historical Society, St. Louis, unless otherwise noted.)

Bernays Collection

De Forest, Lee, Papers of. Lee De Forest Diaries, Vols. 16-23, October 1903-March 1949. Library of Congress Manuscript Division.

Ethical Society of St. Louis Records, Western Historical Manuscript Collection, University of Missouri-St. Louis. (Additional records are stored at Society headquarters in St. Louis County, Mo.)

David R. Francis Papers

Hamilton, Esley. Text accompanying "Louis Clemens Spiering: St. Louis Architect," architectural exhibit at the Sheldon Art Galleries, 1999.

Hemenway, Pamela Gayle. "Cass Gilbert's Buildings at the Louisiana Purchase Exposition, 1904." Master's thesis, University of Missouri, 1970.

Louisiana Purchase Exposition Company Records

Northwestern University Archives, Northwestern University Library

Otis Family Papers, Winnetka Historical Society

Thomas S. Skinker Family Papers

Spiering Family Papers

Louis Spiering correspondence from Paris, collection of the author

Theodore Spiering Scrapbooks, Chicago Historical Society

Index

About *the* **Author**

Enthusiasm for choral singing is what introduced Carol Porter to the Sheldon Concert Hall, leading her to an investigation of its architect and eventually to the authorship of this book. Porter has worked as a freelance journalist and as a magazine editor for institutional publications for the past thirty years. Her features and essays have appeared in Cosmopolitan, *the* St. Louis Post-Dispatch *and the* Chicago Tribune. *Porter is a native of St. Louis, a graduate of University of Missouri School of Journalism and the mother/stepmother of three adult children. She lives in St. Louis County with her husband, Howard Porter, and Oliver, their Yorkshire terrier.*